Fried Chicken
is

Awesome

Finding YOUR way
in a world gone mad

BRAD ALLEN

Published in Ireland 2019.

Published by TPAssist LIMITED.

Copyright Brad Allen 2019.

ISBN 978-1-9162074-1-7

TPAssist LIMITED

14 Penrose Wharf

Cork, T23 CKC8, Ireland

www.tpassist.com

This book is dedicated to these folks;
they became my rock:

John and Lorraine Allen - without their support, all this
would have likely just ended up as mumblings between
my two ears.

Gavin Allen, Janine Hart, Kate Berridge & Peter Day
- for being there for me.

Shelley Crawford, Charlie Stevens & Eleni Demosthenous
- for being true professionals and for the help in creating
the conditions that enabled me to thrive again.

Cover Artwork by Lance Bell of visualisethat.co.uk.

Contents

INTRODUCTION

Chapter 1: Fried Chicken is awesome

Why?

Life has lobbed some awful experiences in my direction. Without a doubt, these focused my attention. However, even before all of that, life was still confusing. I had fun, made progress, achieved things, but there was a sense that something was missing. After the dust settled on the disasters, I realized there was something that I missed from the beginning. I realized that I have always had questions, even when everything seemed to be going okay. I wanted to know if I was doing enough to be a good husband, father, son, friend, co-worker, employee, and manager. I wanted to know if my kids would still want to be around me when they were older. I wanted to know if I was doing enough so that I wouldn't be alone. I wanted to know if what I was doing would ensure that I would have enough money to have a decent living and provide for those I love. I wanted to know if I was doing enough to take care of myself, so I didn't drop dead well before my time.

All these questions pointed to one thing, certainty. I wanted to know with total certainty that I was forging the right path. I wanted to know with total certainty that every choice I made was the right choice to make at that time. What I didn't realize was that, without the right skills, in looking to obtain certainty I was giving up something important. Linked to the lack of certainty is a burden—the burden of my choices. So in effect, the search for what would give me certainty required me to be relieved of the burden of choice. Without a crystal ball to see the future, and with the skills I had at the time, relief from the burden of choice came down to one shocking reality. It meant giving up my ability to choose. Once I stopped making choices or, more importantly, once I stopped taking responsibility for the outcomes, I was freed, and relieved of the burden of choice. However, that freedom came at a huge cost.

I am serious when I say fried chicken is awesome. Your taste might be different, however the world I exist in tells me so many things are bad for me. I hear about things I should or shouldn't do. I exist in a world where I find it challenging if I don't subscribe to what others believe. Finding my way involves being true to what I believe for myself. And I believe fried chicken is awesome. Sure, the first few mouthfuls are the best—the spices, the load of salt, and the grease—and yes, after a few pieces, the anticipation and enjoyment are replaced with a slightly sickly feeling. But that doesn't diminish how good it was at the start. It doesn't take from my intention in putting myself in the same space as the fried chicken. It doesn't take from the fact that I chose to eat it. And, it doesn't stop me from believing in the awesomeness of those first few bites. As for what happens after consuming a bucket, that's a whole different story.

I am a relatively normal guy, who did normal life stuff and still failed to find traction and my place in the madness. I had put everything into my career, my family, and my marriage and yet it still felt like I wasn't getting ahead. I did my best to do all the things I thought were important but the pain and confusion persisted. A lot of the time it felt like swimming against the riptide with diving weights tied to my waist. The advice I came across felt like the joke about the lost tourist asking a farmer for directions to the airport and the farmer responding with "Well, I wouldn't start from here." I explored the classic and popular ways to self-help. I changed careers so I could devote more time to learning about how things should work. I coached, I got coached, and I engaged in counseling/ psychotherapy. I gave attention to understanding how I could get closer to the "right place to start from." Eventually, I got there, but it wasn't the place I expected to be when I started.

In choosing to relinquish my choice to make choices, I got used to being pushed back and shoved out of the way. I let go of who I was and allowed myself to be pushed into the margins, taken advantage of, and tormented for my gullibility. And yet I was often told I was witty, determined, curious, passionate, caring, and empathetic. Eventually I found my way out of that turmoil. The rebuild process uncovered some unexpected strengths. I discovered I was quirky, unconventional and I see the world through strange, and at times edgy, filters. When you bring the painful and disastrous experiences together with these characteristics into the writing of a book, you get something that is unique, magic, ground-breaking, and of great value to all it touches. That is who I am and that is what this book is.

Being authentic

The title of this book has a hidden message. If we take the "F" and the "C" from the "Fried Chicken" and say it quickly you get "Feck." You can use another variation of Feck also, if you like. I'll stay with Feck. Now if we drop the "s" from "is" and add an "am" to make it work grammatically, and leave "Awesome" where it is, you get "Feck I am Awesome."

The real magic, the trick, and the key that this book leverages, is that we need to truly believe "Feck I am Awesome." I am not talking about me, Brad. I am talking about you. Equally, I am not talking about ego-driven narcissists who think they are awesome, when they are not. No, I'm talking about the truth that comes from the heart, that "I" have all that I need.

Truly believing I was awesome was not part of me for a very long time. I can't remember when I started to doubt myself—perhaps as I got into adolescence. Thankfully, I made it through, eventually. The glimmer of hope and sense that there was more to it all, helped me stay with the journey. And that is all I really needed, the hope and the desire to keep searching. With this belief firmly entrenched in my psyche, I behaved authentically, and that is where the real joy, wonder, and meaning was found.

This book is about being authentic, (i.e., the process of using our truth to create wonderful, productive, and engaging experiences for ourselves and others). This book looks at the individual experience of authenticity, which for most of us is a continual challenge. There are two opposing ideas at play when we talk about being authentic. On one hand, I want to be myself and align to my own purpose and identity. On the other hand, by my nature, I want to be social and be part of something. That requires me to compromise and be part of someone else's purpose and identity. However, if I try too hard to be part of someone else's reality, those others can't benefit from the uniqueness that I bring. This is further complicated because from an early age I was conditioned to be aware of my impact on others. So, if I say and do exactly what I feel is right for me at every moment, I will inevitably offend someone else. That limits my ability to be social and benefit from what others can offer me, while if I constantly filter what I say and do, I corrupt my responses, and that impacts my ability to experience the world as I want to experience it. Being authentic, therefore, is both a balancing act of satisfying my own needs and the needs of others, as well as a battle to understand my conditioning and use it to help me, not inhibit me.

Being authentic is where it both feels right and is right. Being authentic is when there is close to no resistance in my mind to what I say, do, and experience. It is when I get what I want without compromising myself or others. It is when the burdens I carry feel almost weightless. When that happens, I sense The Light. The Light is the gel that seamlessly brings the right things together at the right time. For some, this could be thought of as divine intervention. Some speak of personal power. Some refer to it as intuition. Some look to their sixth sense. Some use objects. Some think of it as the way of the universe. Some use the term pure love. Star Wars geeks like me will call it The Force. Whatever the label, to read this book, and appreciate the numerous examples in subsequent chapters, think of it as the thing that helps us on our journey. It's the intangible sense that surrounds us and guides us.

Resistance

When I do or experience something in the present moment that honors my current self but has detrimental consequences for my future self, I am creating unnecessary resistance. A simplistic example would be eating a lot of chocolate cake. It has engagement in the present moment, however if I don't make use of the excess sugars, I am creating problems for my future self in the form of unnecessary weight gain.

When I do or experience something in the present moment that both honors my current self and has only positive consequences for my future self, I reduce the resistance. For example, when I just have one piece of chocolate cake, which is proportionate to what I have recently eaten and my immediate plans to make use of the sugars, I don't create problems for my future self.

Authenticity is not about trying to eliminate the resistance entirely; that's just not how the universe works. It's the resistance, the uncertainty, which creates the experience. The trick is to be aware of the resistance and manage it well. Once I do that, I am being authentic. Even if I am doing something that seems to be very brave, failure to acknowledge the resistance puts me in the passenger seat. At that point I am not being authentic. When I don't sense and acknowledge the resistance, I am in denial of it. A good way to look at resistance is by looking at fear. While resistance is created from all our negative emotions, like disgust, boredom, hate, envy, sorrow, anger, frustration, discontentment, alarm, guilt, indifference, it is fear where we can see it clearly. To understand light, you must have dark. To understand authenticity, you must have resistance. To understand the resistance, we can explore the fear that holds us back: the fear of putting our views forward; the fear of asking for what we need; the fear of going after something we want; the fear of saying no, or the fear of letting go of something we have. Resistance isn't really about effort or work. There will always be things we don't feel like doing but must do, like cleaning the house, medical check-ups, or sharing sad news. At the core of the resistance is a conflict in my mind and heart as to the alignment of the experience to what I feel is right for myself and for those I care about.

Context

We exist in a world gone mad. Sure, we have famine, war, exploitation, and all manner of things going wrong. That's not what I'm talking about. These awful truths have been present since the beginning of our existence. Life has been hard and unfair for a very long time. For as long as we can recall, we have had thinkers and doers, leaders and followers, heroes and scoundrels, hard workers and thieves. None of that is new and none of it suggests a change of anything for better or worse. The thing that has gone mad is the experience of ourselves within the world. I risk filling my time with greater amounts of things that don't really matter. I risk draining my thinking capacity in a search for

7

things to blame and find wrong with everything and everyone else. I risk focusing every moment possible on the pursuit of getting as close as I can to becoming a perfect superhuman being. I can berate myself for lack of understanding of what it all means. It is these things that are new and that are not right.

I chose the path that led to this book because I truly want to make my own choices and define my own path. While it took time, I realized I wanted something more. I no longer wanted to be a drone, entertaining myself to pass the time until I take my final breath. I wanted a better experience of life for myself and the generations that follow. I wanted to see less friction in my interactions with loved ones, my communities, and within my workplaces. I went searching for a better experience of the world and a better understanding of my place in it. I didn't find a magic wand or some wonderfully simple seven-step plan. What I found was unexpected but relatively obvious. I don't have all the answers. I still face challenges. I still find myself blindsided on idle Tuesdays. I still must work hard to be and get what I need and want. However, so much more of it makes sense to me now. There is no burden, and yet I am making my own choices. There is less friction and there is less resistance, across all spectrums of my life.

I wouldn't change a thing. Every decision and experience got me to this point. Sure, I could have done things differently or "better" to avoid certain challenges and pain for me and others. I even swam across a stretch of water once, in the middle of the night, with my clothes and shoes held high in the air just to avoid having to admit I was wrong about the departure time of the last ferry. Perhaps different decisions could have allowed me to accumulate more stuff, see more places, or experienced more. Ultimately the choices I made, created the journey that got me here, and I love the place I am at now.

I've been lucky, in that I haven't endured chronic physical pain. Sure, I've struggled with back pain, had injuries, and had ingrown hairs where they shouldn't be. Some of that was excruciatingly painful. However, it wasn't the end of the earth. I've been blessed when it comes to facing real physical challenges. On the other hand, I've been to the edge, mentally, and suffered emotional pain like there was no way out.

It's funny in a way, when we look back. I certainly must force myself to laugh at times to keep the anger and frustration in check, and to help keep the waterworks at bay. As a young adult when I imagined my future, that future didn't include putting my career and physical wellbeing on hold to support my partner and raise my children. When it happened, I somehow thought that I'd get emotional and financial recognition for the years of effort. I lived with the delusion that if I shared my grievances and concerns with those who I thought had my back, they would support me. I had come to believe recessions didn't impact me and that I'd never struggle to make ends meet. I figured family law was there to protect the innocent. I naively believed family law would treat fathers and mothers equally, and not just hear what fits with what everyone expects. All these stupid misconceptions left me angry and frustrated. It left me blaming others for the lack of meaning. It left me staring into the abyss and idealizing launching into it. Some have said that I've been there and back, mentally.

For more years than I like to admit I felt stalled, and found it hard to rationalize what had gone wrong, but I endured. The years of torment nearly broke me, but I kept getting into life, one day at a time. I fought to get my head back together and bring my body along with me. Through it all, I put on a brave face and kept smiling. I reinvented myself; I created a new career as a coach and facilitator, and I fought hard to get access to my children so I could continue to be the great father that they need. It hasn't been easy and it's an ongoing journey. These reflections are not a search for sympathy, nor am I trying to impress you. I am, however, hopefully creating a level of credibility for the ideas I share in this book. The more time I spent exploring my experience, the more I realized I am not unique in any measure. My experience is endured repeatedly, by many, many people. It's for this reason that I decided to share the things I've learned along the way, in a hope that my learning could in some way, even if only in a small measure, help others.

Ready?

This book contains a series of guided self-coaching topics. These are the things I have learned along my journey. Some things were taught to me; however, most have been learned from mistakes and often far too much stubborn blindness. The self-coaching topics are supported by observations about my behavior and experiences, as well as those of people that I have worked with as a coach, mentor, and facilitator.

As I will explore further in chapter twenty, my view of the world is not conventional. While I am normal in that I share with others the many failings and strengths that make up the human experience, there is one strength that I share with only a few. Some mistake this trait for laziness, or perfectionism, or even a compulsive disorder. I've compared myself to others and naively felt entitled because they didn't exhibit this strength. The reality is that I am simply incredibly curious about the effort and choices we make in order to realize outcomes. That curiousness drives so much of how I engage with the world. It has led me through many experiences, some joyful, and many more, painful. From the observations of these experiences, I've drawn tips and tricks that have helped me and others get closer to projecting authentic selves.

This book contains more than two dozen self-coaching topics, spread across four themes. In Part 1, I explore how limiting beliefs and associated behaviors let me down, specifically when I am with others. In Part 2, I focus on the idea of realistic optimism and how it provides a better approach to making choices. In Part 3, I explore thinking, emotions, socializing, and the physical aspects of the personal experience of engaging with life. The final part of the book is where I share what helped me create momentum. This section of the book aims to dive deeply into the potential of the ideas shared in Parts 1 through 3. This final section of the book is really about The Light. I share what worked for me in finding it, understanding it, and staying in it.

Some of those who had early knowledge of my ideas for this book shared their beliefs that this material may well disturb and change people, and that most people wouldn't be ready for what I share. My aim with this material is to invoke strong emotions, though I hope it's not seen as disturbing by too many. I do hope it helps fuel change and I agree that lots aren't ready. While this material is for anyone, it's not for everyone. Conditioning leaves some unable to see their experiences as opportunities for learning. Without a learner's mindset, the contents of this book have the potential to be used simply to justify limiting behavior or find labels to blame.

A note of caution: While the books that I will mention do have references to research, I am not the type to need hard evidence before I test and explore a theory. So you won't find me preoccupied with including that. I can only suggest that if you read something here that is new to you, instead of looking for external evidence, ask yourself this simple question—"how does this feel for me?" And, if it feels right, then keep reading.

Finally, don't take anything here too seriously. Enjoy it. Learn from it. However, it's my journey and my learning, not yours. Test and explore what I've learned, but take it all at face value.

PART 1:
BE TRUE TO
YOURSELF

Chapter 2: Hands off! The fish batter and skin on the chicken is mine!

Battered fish

In a life spent lost in the course of time and learning experiences, I was confused and misaligned. I felt powerful and accomplished, but I was unhappy. As a young adult, I left home for a job and rarely looked back. For several years, the time I spent with my family was short and intense, during the typical occasions that families gather, like during the holiday season. It was during one of these rare visits, that I made things harder for myself.

At the time I felt I was in a relatively good place. I was on a search for improvement and I was committed to answering some of the big questions. During this visit, I went with my parents, siblings, and our partners, to a pub restaurant for lunch. Their specialty was freshly caught fish, and it was served battered with delicious chunky chips. We ordered drinks and food and we were catching up on each other's lives. There was lots of laughter and good quality banter. When my plate of mouth-watering fish and chips arrived, without a second thought I proceeded to remove the batter from my fish. I didn't think anything was amiss until I noticed the shock and horror on the faces of my family. They weren't seeing the Brad they knew. (To be clear, growing up we ate simple foods, mostly at home. Meals were generally balanced and wholesome. However, we also appreciated there was a time and a place for treats.)

It was one of the fittest periods of my life up to that point. I wasn't on a specific diet, but I was watching what I ate. The incident quickly passed with some jokes and new conversation to distract everyone. Their shock was because they knew me. They knew I would have wanted to eat the fish as the chef had intended it to be eaten, and believe me, I did. They were confused as to why I had removed the batter, as was I. I was on a track that was someone else's. I hadn't given it a second thought until that point. It left a mark on me and became a significant catalyst for my search for why and how I compromise my authenticity.

The behavior of removing batter, and other similar forms, like skin on fried chicken, was not my own. I had adopted the behavior from those I was socializing with. I thought it was important because they were doing it. When I allowed myself to adopt this behavior, I gave up my autonomy. I gave up a little piece of my authenticity and replaced it with someone else's. Adopting someone else's beliefs and, behaviors, without question, takes my choices away.

Permission

Adopting the beliefs and behaviors of others isn't a bad thing, so long as I understand the reasons and choose it for myself. However, there lie dangers within. When I mimic others, it can be perceived as giving permission to take further liberties. Before I know it, my choices are being taken away without any negotiation. And this is where the damage can be done. This is where I find it hard to be true to myself.

It can hurt, or at the least break my flow, when someone takes my choices away. When someone does something in my name it must be something that aligns with what I want. Otherwise, it doesn't feel right. It is even harder when that action is done with a smile and is in a context where confrontation causes further stress. When done well, the behavior has all the indications of genuine concern. When it isn't. It's just being manipulative or needy, and it is simply bullying.

Bullying takes many forms. Someone going behind my back and using lies or half-truths to manipulate situations to suit their own needs is one form. However, the behavior can be just as effective in plain sight if the perpetrator has enough skills to hide their intentions. Controlling, manipulative, and needy behavior is satirized brilliantly by Patricia Routledge paying the role of Hyacinth Bucket, aka Mrs Bucket, in Roy Clarke's British sitcom, *Keeping Up Appearances*. Mrs Bucket is obvious in her misguided meddling.

The deeper and more disturbing form of bullying comes when it's hard to discern if someone is really trying to help or if they are being manipulative. Passive-aggressive behavior, indirect manipulation and resistance, has a public form. Acting in plain sight of others creates a smoke screen that hides the truth. The action may be hurtful, or it may involve giving a compliment or advice that appears to be constructive and in my interest, when it is really something I don't agree with.

An example might be when a manager tells the team that "Mal wants help finishing the sales pitch," when Mal knows the manager simply doesn't agree with the direction Mal is taking. The manager wants to appear empathetic and empowering, not controlling and interfering. If Mal speaks up and contradicts the manager, Mal will look petty, and silly. Another example might be when a partner disagrees with their significant other about the use of lights in the house. At a dinner party they might casually say something like "Kim loves the brightness and turns lights on all over the house." And, one final example might be when a committee member is annoyed with another member for not agreeing to help lobby a change in the time of a meeting. The annoyed member might say in front of Val and the group, "Val is very busy, juggling lots of really important work." It's hard for others to know what's really going on, unless they have deep knowledge of the background and relationship of the bully and person being bullied.

I have seen these behaviors in all kinds of places. The impact on my enjoyment and experience has been severely compromised when I haven't been able to handle this abusive behavior. I know that when I continue to give up my autonomy and give permission for my choices to be made by someone else, I risk becoming alienated and marginalized.

The artist

It is one thing to allow someone to blatantly reduce my choices; it's another thing altogether to invite it. In my mid-thirties I did a contract with a large utility. It was a consulting role, so I was very much an outsider. I already had experience of working in large bureaucracies, however I still was naive when it came to passive manipulative behaviors. One of the people I worked with had a habit of over-committing and under-delivering. Unfortunately for me, he was not as naive as I was. He knew exactly what was needed to cover his tracks.

In the beginning, I aligned with his approach. I thought he was cool. I admired his calmness and appearance of all knowing and intelligence. I adopted his approach, putting what I felt was better aside. It was functional, colorful, and detailed. It was very aligned to what I enjoyed. However, the enjoyment was short lived. As we'd say in Australia, "I was a flaming idiot."

When things went off the rails, which they did regularly, I'd do my best to manage things around him. I would further compromise my work to make up for his failing. And yet, I still did my best to do things his way. The effort took away from me doing what I was there to do and what I was good at. Eventually I changed tack and tried alerting him to the undersight or oversight. He would ignore me and then bring the conversation up during meetings, or in the corridors, and always when others were present. He'd use what I had shared privately about our shortcomings and mistakes. He would offer to help me in some way unrelated to the challenge at hand, thus shifting the focus away from himself. To all those who would listen, he'd share what actions he had taken to help me out, none of which would have been what we agreed or what we needed. When I tried to confront him, he would listen calmly and pleasantly. Then as I was getting increasingly upset with his lack of response, he would simply ask, "What exactly are you saying, Brad?" which is impossible to answer if you have already gone to great lengths to explain yourself. Understandably, my contract with that firm didn't go beyond its original term. It was a frustrating time. However, I learned a valuable lesson. I learned that aligning with someone else's values and beliefs only takes me further away from my potential.

The helpful

Even harder still is when the manipulation is subtle. It makes it harder to detect and avoid. We all have experienced someone who is always doing "helpful" things for others without being asked. They are usually the first ones to pop over with a tray of lasagna when someone is sick or there is a bereavement. Without my soliciting assistance they'll do things at work "for me," but not in a way that really helps me. They buy me things I don't need. And as they are doing all of those "helpful" deeds, they expect accolades at the time and then use sweetness to bully their way into favors later. Just before asking for my help they'll ask me about that book they got me last month. They go out of their way to be interested in things I am doing, e.g., they'll take a keen interest in my movements. Then, when I indicate a gap in my schedule, they'll suddenly have an idea. Usually it is something they need, and it will, astonishingly, fit precisely into my schedule gap. I get stuck with no way out. They already know I can't turn them down because they know I don't have any commitments at that time. While they will suggest otherwise, all of this will be in their best interest, not mine. They will be reluctant to ask openly for my help, because they want to avoid any sense that they owe me. They want to stay in control. They will go to efforts so that it looks like they are doing me a favor by giving me something worthwhile to fill my spare time. They do this to make it look like whatever it is, it's for my benefit not theirs. Then if I do find something that I need their help with, they will make all kinds of seemingly legitimate excuses and then over-enthusiastically promise to help "next time." Of course, I'm not suggesting this applies to everyone that turns up with a tray of lasagna or does things we didn't ask for. Thankfully, many acts like these are done with an honest interest in giving and expecting nothing in return.

Enjoying the meal

My faith in the human experience tells me that often these types of behaviors aren't with malicious intent, just misguided. That misdirection is often simply someone following, without question, a path and set of behaviors defined by someone else, like a parent or teacher. They are all simply lemmings merrily on their way to the edge of the cliff. This is the basis of what I call a "borrowed belief." More of that later. At all times I simply need to look for what doesn't feel right and look for what is important to me. I need to eat the batter on the fish or skin on the fried chicken, if I feel it is right. I need to distance myself from those who try to compromise my choices. I need to get better skills to confront those that I must endure. I must find the space needed to stay true to what I believe and value.

Chapter 3: Embrace vulnerability

Holding back

Relationships are a troublesome necessity. Research shows us that we need them, but my goodness—it's hard to figure them out. The same relationship can give us the most amazing experience, as well as the most dreadful. Relationships start at the first moment we meet someone, be it in person or via an electronic exchange. The quality of the relationship can be built over small or long periods. It isn't clear what always works and what always fails. It's a terribly confusing part of my existence. When I engage in an interaction with someone new, the quality and outcomes will largely depend on my state of mind (i.e., if I am open and accepting), I am more likely to experience something real and rich. On the other hand, if I am fearful and judgmental, I am likely to experience something that leaves me frustrated, blaming, and somewhat underwhelmed.

My secondary education was typical for a middle-class person in the 1980s in a prosperous Christian country. It focused primarily on reading, writing, math, science, and religion, and somewhat on history, geography, art, language, and technology. There was little to do with learning about any sort of relationship building, be it intimate, or otherwise. The education taught me not to look too deeply because I might find some things that don't quite add up and ask difficult questions. That was presented to me as being bad and dangerous, because I must put my faith in those that know better. So I was left to explore and educate myself in how to do relationships properly, via movies, and somewhat awkward and superficial conversations with my friends. As a consequence, I found building relationships, limiting and frustrating.

When I finally had the self-confidence to return to exploring what it all means, I found something obvious, but challenging. It became clear to me that to achieve fulfilling relationships, there needed to be a willingness to share, ask, and be asked, the difficult questions. I needed to embrace vulnerability.

When I hold back, I compromise the potential. This comes in many forms, like holding back what I truly think or believe is important, as we explored in Chapter two. Another form would be presenting a version of myself that is not me; but is what I think the other person wants to see and experience. We will explore this further in Chapter four. A further form would be second-guessing what the other person wants before I share, rather than just sharing or asking them. A simple example of this would be agreeing to have a glass of wine when I really want a peppermint tea. All these forms of holding back are defense mechanisms based on fear of ridicule, rejection and getting hurt. They hide my true desires, wants and needs. Holding back protects me but blocks me from learning and growing. However, if I am comfortable sharing and learning about my vulnerabilities, I open the door to connection.

It is easy to tell myself and anyone who wants to listen, that my relationships are working, and things are going to be okay. Unfortunately, only one of those statements is guaranteed to be true. Solid and lasting relationships require effort. There is plenty of evidence to suggest that most long-term relationships, particularly marriage, aren't working. However, it is true that things are going to be okay, the simple truth being that things will work out, even if the relationship doesn't. The key here is to accept the reality and do my best to move to a place where everything is okay. Thankfully, that might also include the relationship.

The yacht

I like to think of starting a relationship as being like buying a yacht together, be that relationship with colleagues, a future mate, sports teams, or acquaintances. I can picture you reading this and thinking, "what has this got to do with finding my way". Perhaps you are thinking, "I would never want to buy a yacht even if I could afford it". You may even have gone to, "I don't have the foggiest of how to sail; how is this relevant?" All these are valid thoughts, so for now I ask that you indulge me and use your imagination or, if that's not happening, picture someone else starting a new relationship as you read. Whatever type of relationship, or type, and size of the boat or ship involved, the process and eventuality is relatively similar. For the yacht to be reliable it needs to be maintained. The same is true of productive and long-lasting relationships.

When you take delivery of your new shiny yacht, you might ease yourselves into it slowly. You might take it out and about in relatively calm waters. You will test it somewhat and get used to making it move well. You will have some fun, just us, enjoying this new thing. You won't be on the yacht all the time. You will park it back in the marina and go off and do your own things at times. Then at other times, you won't be alone (i.e., you might sail with others in a flotilla of yachts).

Like all new things, new yachts don't need much maintenance at the start. You simply get into it, drive on, and have fun. However, over time things break. Perhaps it might be pushed a little too hard or run too close to something. Then after a while, perhaps there is a need for a new coat of paint/varnish or some repairs to the woodwork. Perhaps the sails and engine need repairing or servicing. Further down the line, the yacht might need to be taken out of the water and given some major repairs to strengthen the superstructure to carry more (i.e., a larger team or new family members). This also might be necessary so that the yacht performs well in more difficult waters (e.g., economic downturns, ill-health, changing environments).

Even when new things come with user manuals, who reads them? It's more likely that getting to know your yacht is based on trial and error, and perhaps some training if you are a little organized and forward thinking. Learning to make the most of the yacht is relatively easy, in that it's something that has immediate and more tangible benefits. Mastering the art of maintaining the yacht might be a little harder for most, simply because, it is harder to apply the discipline to learning and doing something when the benefits are only realized down the track. Furthermore, since this is a shared endeavor, your ability to effectively and efficiently work together will be highly dependent on what you know about your own abilities and strengths. If you only have an inkling of what each can bring to the table, you might waste energy trying to do something that someone else can already do better. This learning, or appreciation of who you are, will have a direct impact on how much you get out of the new thing. This appreciation of who you are will also impact how well you do the more difficult job of maintenance.

When you sail into troubled waters, any lack of maintenance becomes more evident (i.e., if the hull leaks or the hatches and windows don't close properly), you run the risk of sinking. Equally, if the engine doesn't work properly or the sails are torn or worn out, they won't push the yacht at the speed needed to successfully get through the storm. And finally, if you haven't fully explored and developed your understanding of what abilities and strengths each has, you may lose your heads or fail to take the actions needed to weather the storm.

Sailing successfully through any weather, be it calm or rough, is down to preparation. The more you know about the capabilities of the yacht and yourselves, the higher the probability that you will get where you want to be and have a great time as you do it. Preparation is both learning and hard work (i.e., maintenance). Yacht-ownership-related learning is about understanding the physical elements and using physical tools. Relationship-related learning is about knowing what you value and what your individual strengths are. The best way to build that understanding is to be open and honest with each other by accepting vulnerability and stop holding back.

Sparks cause fires

Cracks in relationships become more prevalent and are harder to fix when there is insufficient investment and preparation. Relationships are often talked about as starting with a "spark" or being "hot" and then having lost their "fire." Let's look at fires for a moment, specifically bushfires. Forest and bushfires are a major problem in many parts of the world. The dry and hot climate is a very fertile place for rampant and uncontrollable bushfires that put property and lives at risk. At times during the year, no open fires are allowed. During the cooler and wetter times of the year, great efforts are made to clear firebreaks, keep grass low, and back-burn tracks of land. All this preparation is to help prevent and manage fires during the dry season.

The threat of fire comes from all corners. Some are started through neglect and failure to adhere to the fire ban. Some are purposely lit by disturbed individuals. Others are caused naturally, e.g., through lightning strikes. While potentially catastrophic, fires aren't all bad. In fact, many of the indigenous trees and plants have become so accustomed to the fires that they have evolved ways to regrow. Some ecosystems totally rely on the fires to prevent overgrowth and thus create the right conditions for survival. These ecosystems can rebuild themselves from the ashes and thrive. The damage caused by the fire makes the whole system stronger. This is the same with relationships. Conflict under the right conditions and with the right preparation can make the relationship stronger. However, conflict in the ill-prepared relationship can be terminal.

Things get harder in relationships as we take on more complexity, e.g., children, aging parents, the aging process, or less than perfect careers. If we don't work hard to keep on top of things, the relationship struggles and eventually breaks.

I love my children to bits; I have no regrets about the choice I made to be a father and wouldn't want to be without them in my life. However, there is no doubt in my mind that having them was like a wildfire in my relationship with their mother. The spark that created the magic and the children turned against us, and caused havoc within our relationship. Unfortunately, we were ill-prepared, and not evolved to such a point that the fire enabled new growth.

The three Cs

To succeed, all relationships must involve attention to the three Cs: chemistry, cognitive alignment, and context, intimate relationships even more so. Without attention to these three aspects, relationships have faltered and drained my energy.

Chemistry is obvious, but often neglected. For non-intimate relationships, I need to enjoy sharing the same space as the people I am spending time with. This doesn't mean I am physically attracted to them; it simply means I don't get repulsed by their look or their smell or their outward behaviors. With intimate relationships, I need to truly lust for them. That doesn't always happen. Perhaps there is a degree of desperation, perhaps there is something about the intimacy that is new and exciting, perhaps ego is telling me they will look good on my arm. Unfortunately, a compromise here will be fatal later. While perhaps neglected, chemistry is the easiest to get right. The test is simple. All I need to consider is am I totally attracted to this person when they are at their worst, physically? For example, consider this when I meet them during or at the end of an exhausting day, stressed and preoccupied, does the sign of the other person bring on an immediate smile? If the answer is yes, then the chemistry is solid. If I only find myself physically attracted to them when they are looking their best, things aren't how they should be. It's true that over time I might get a little too comfortable and take less care of myself than I should. Nevertheless, even as I grow old, become less firm, gain or lose hair and get a little more rounded, the core of the beauty will remain and that's what creates the chemistry. Without the chemistry I am just pretending. It's like playing golf with plastic balls or drinking non-alcoholic beer at a wine tasting. Embracing vulnerability helps ensure there is honesty in how I physically relate to those I want to spend time with.

Cognitive alignment is crucial for longevity, but not so important in flings and for superficial relationships. Cognitive alignment includes aspects of personality and how we interact with the world. For longevity, relationships need to have alignment in sense of humor, similar levels of emotional intelligence, some similar interests, and a degree of alignment of ideologies and other life philosophies. Sense of humor is the most important of all these aspects and is likely to be aligned from the start. This is, of course, if I am being honest with myself and not just letting my primal urges drive my laughter even when I don't get the other person's humor. Life is hard but it will become unbearable if I am not sharing laughter at myself and the world.

A similar level of emotional intelligence is important so I can relate properly. Emotional intelligence is something I grow. It's not fixed, but I need to start a relationship with someone at a similar level so one isn't having to educate or bring the other person on. Having a teacher-and-student dynamic can be fun in aspects of a relationship, but it gets tiresome if it's one-sided all the time.

Similar interests create opportunities for shared experiences. It's during those shared experiences that laughter is found, and learning takes place.

Finally, having some degree of alignment in ideologies and other life philosophies ensures the next world conflict doesn't breakout on the first date. Alignment here ensures I have things to share that I am passionate about.

Context is the facts of my being that exist at the start of a relationship. These will include: my habits and routines; my physical condition; my mental condition; my commitments to work, family, and friends; my financial flexibility; my baggage, and my skills in managing complexity. Whatever the stage of life I am at when I meet someone, I will always have context. This context will both enable and get in the way of a strong and lasting relationship. Lack of flexibility in many of these aspects will stop me meeting the right people. When I do meet someone, inflexibility makes it harder to experience each other fully. It just isn't realistic that I will be able to keep everything the same after I meet someone. I am going to need to make changes. I might need to spend less time with some of my friends or family, to make room for the new person. I might need to change some of my routines and habits to fit better with their availability. I might need to invite them into my existing activities and share then with them. I might need to work on my physical condition so that we can have better sex. I might need to seek help to remove more of the baggage. I might need to reduce my financial security somewhat, so I have the means to engage fully in new and shared experiences. An unwillingness to share and integrate new people into existing routines, experiences, and friendships keeps them out.

Of the three Cs, while all are necessary, cognitive alignment is the most important. Having the ability to connect with each other on similar emotional and intellectual levels enables us to learn about each other's needs, our individual contexts, and is required to create the new and shared conditions necessary for rich and lasting relationships.

The potential of the union

While healthy intimate relations are very important, this chapter is about more than that. Embracing vulnerability works both literally and figuratively. It is about how I approach relationships of any kind. When I put my perceptions in between me and others, I limit the potential for rich and rewarding cognitive and physical unions. When I am not authentic in relationships, the trust is harder to build. The secrets I hold on to keep me from reaching my potential. When I am allowing my authentic self to shine through, my relationships grow, and thrive. The combined unions become nothing short of magic.

Chapter 4: Peel off the labels

Named brands

Thankfully my childhood wasn't focused on named brands. We weren't lacking the necessities, but we didn't have a lot of new stuff. I had no concept of named brands. A new bike was a new bike. A new t-shirt was a new t-shirt. It didn't matter the brand or who else had one the same. I don't feel that lack of awareness was due to lack of means, because I don't remember my envy being brand related. I do remember envying some of the stuff other kids had, but it was the type of stuff, not the brand. In my late twenties I was made aware by those I was socializing with, that I was wearing generic brand clothing. I hadn't given it much thought until that point. The more I immersed in that new circle of friends, the more I realized what a brilliant job the marketing industry had done on these people. And it wasn't just a few, it was a whole nation. A nation that went from having nothing to having lots. The brilliant minds in the consumer goods industry had capitalized on it. It felt good to be recognized and be accepted as part of this new group, so I joined them, and became brand-aware. It amuses me now to reflect. Items that I bought for myself, or items that were gifted to me from this new community, were big named brands, while items gifted to me from family members still weren't.

I since stopped buying clothing and related goods because of the label. I now buy because of need, function, and quality. The process of understanding my behavior in relation to brand labels has been useful in understanding how I perceive myself. This is the idea that I am defined by the badge on my shirt or car. It's a crazy notion really, but it was my existence for a long time. I found I defined myself based on what others thought or saw, not by who I felt I was.

The personality test

When I was in my second-last year of high school, I did a personality test. I did it in a class and we all got a definition of our personality. The teacher did his best to prepare us for the test and then help us understand what it meant. Perhaps I wasn't listening or perhaps the teacher missed something important.

However, I didn't appreciate that the results only showed how we represented and perceived ourselves at that moment in time. I took the results as a definition of who I was. I have since lost the copy of the results, but I clearly remember the one piece that stuck with me. The piece that I remember suggested I was a "quiet extrovert." I remember the teacher saying that "quiet" meant that I wouldn't speak up first, and, that "extroverted" meant that I liked to be the center of attention. I clung onto that first piece and pushed aside the second aspect. The idea that I didn't speak up gave me license not to share my ideas. It gave me license to sit back and let others do all the talking. I used it to hold myself back.

At the time, I didn't fully understand what extraversion meant, but I latched onto the idea of "center of attention" and that it wasn't a good thing. My childhood conditioning had told me that I shouldn't be demanding or asked for more than I deserve. I started to believe that being the center of attention was a bad thing and should be avoided. I applied myself not to be the center of attention. The results of bringing both aspects together meant that I didn't speak up, and I avoided or pushed away any sign of my getting attention. I became introverted without realizing it. I became what I thought the results told me about myself. I stopped looking to be myself. I did further similar personality tests through tertiary study and as my career progressed, however none stuck with me so vividly as this single exercise in my mid-teens.

In the early stages of moving into coaching, I did formal training in administering and using these psychometric-based personality tests. The thing that struck me at that point was how naive I had been back in secondary school. I discovered that there are lots of different tests. Every one of these has its benefits and limitations. Many of the tests are based on traditional psychology and stem from the work by Carl Jung and others in the early twentieth century. Traditional psychology is, in simplistic terms, the study of those that don't fit with what society sees as having normal behaviors. This is different from positive psychology. Positive psychology, in simplistic terms, studies those that society sees as succeeding and being happier and more balanced than that of the average person. Jung's works have been extended and have crossed over with a number of other researchers, the most well known being the Myers–Briggs Type Indicator (MBTI). This test gives you an indication of your personality by how you perceive your world and your interaction with it and others. It is therefore self-reflective and relevant to what is going on for you at that moment in time. While it is self-reflective and based on the given moment, with open and honest answers it does provide some good insights. Equally, the test does do its best to catch attempts to mislead the results by asking the same question in several different ways. However, with practice and good knowledge of how the test works, the test taker can sway the results in the direction they want. This isn't helpful for recruiters using the tests as part of employee placement. Nor is it useful if I want to really understand more about myself. In Part 3, I explore better ways to build understanding of who I am.

Labeling

When someone calls me handsome or gorgeous, my reaction is based on the labels I have for those words. In addition, the meaning I place on the words will be subject to other factors, like who said it, my relationship to that person, how they said it, and who else heard it. If it was someone I just started working for and in front of my new colleagues, would I find it offensive and patronizing? Would it cause me discomfort and dramatically reduce my ability to perform? On the other hand, if it was an intimate partner shortly after passionate sex, how would I respond? Would I see it as a turn-on or turn-off? These are trivial examples and easily understood. However, what if the context wasn't as clear? What if the word handsome or gorgeous came from someone I work with in a private setting and I was massively attracted to that person? It gets murky. Equally, what if the word handsome or gorgeous came from someone I'd only recently met socially? It gets equally murky. Consider if I had been conditioned to believe the word handsome or gorgeous has patronizing connotations, no matter what the context or tone. And consider if the other person believed something completely different. Perhaps they believed it was more of a general greeting and didn't hide any underlying intentions. Would things get harder for me if I get unnecessarily upset with a new boss and in a culture that uses the terms openly without any real associated meaning? And what of the person I had just met socially? How would I choose to respond? What if I responded negatively and defensively? Would I reduce my chances of a meaningful encounter and perhaps miss the opportunity to create a wonderful friendship or finally find love?

I have many failings. I have many strengths. We all do. However, only a few others share my approach to the human experience. It took many frustrating years trying to understand this. I even created labels for those that didn't share my passion. I called them "Average Joes," or simply "AJs." As a consultant, this showed up often in my interactions with others, selling and delivering services. I allowed myself to get frustrated at others who didn't have their things organized. I would find myself annoyed with those who didn't seem too concerned about over-committing and under-delivering. I'd find it frustrating sending those "friendly" reminders for the commitments we made together. I labeled them as "average" because I felt they failed to understand the negative impact on our relationship for their lack of attention or responsiveness. The irony, of course, is that I am average, as are we all. This limiting view of human nature just brings pain and frustration. As I will explore further in chapter twenty, I simply couldn't rationalize why everyone wasn't as keen as I was to ensure everything they did, or experienced, was always about the right things being done the right way.

Using "always" or "never"

Not all labels hold us back, but we can achieve more engagement and richer experiences if we identify those that do. It is not easy to understand fully which labels are working for me or against me. A method that has worked for me is to observe how and when I use absolutes like "always" or "never."

As an example, I ask myself if any of these phrases feature in my conversations:

I always think/feel/say/do/have/buy/wear BLANK.

I never think/feel/say/do/have/buy/wear BLANK.

For each of these BLANKs, I ask "why," (i.e., "Why do I always do BLANK?") When I get the answer, I reflect on the origins. I see if I still feel the same now. If the answer includes an "always" or "never," I think harder (i.e., "I always wear blue, because I always have" isn't a reasonable answer). And, I look out for using someone or something else as the justification, (i.e., "I always do it that way, because my father did it that way"). This is a borrowed belief, which we will explore in lots of detail in chapter six.

Referring to my earlier example, for a long time when asked "why don't you speak up?" my reply would have been "because I'm a quiet extrovert." I wouldn't share where I got that notion. However, the high school assessment and my teacher's comments were always just there in my mind as I gave the answer. It was a label I applied to myself, and it held me back.

It is likely that, if I can't provide my own answer to the why, I am not allowing my true self to be surfaced. Asking this of myself will help surface if it's a label that I might want to peel off.

Chapter 5: You don't have to speak to the person next to you

Talking to the person next to you is a choice; it's not mandatory. Silence is often a far better option.

Planes, trains, and buses

Having spent many hours traveling on planes, trains, and buses over the years, I often felt uncomfortable with the idea of engaging with the person next to me. I would get stressed about starting a conversation. I would be relieved when the seat next to me was empty.

When I didn't work up the courage to engage, I would carry guilt for hours and sometimes, days later. I would think about the "what Ifs?" I would think about what would have happened if I had engaged in a conversation. I would try to justify my lack of engagement with saying to myself, "I was saved." I rationalized that if I got started there would have been no turning back if the conversation was boring, painful, or simply annoying. What I failed to notice was that other people rarely started conversations either. It sounds absurd now that I think about it.

When I did manage to have a conversation, it was usually quite pleasant but not anything life changing. I had the belief that this was because I was stressed during the conversation, too concerned about what to say. This all got me thinking. Was I unique in the concerns and guilt I carried, or was there something more here to explore?

Learning about silence

In my thirties, I helped sell and deliver Information Technology services. Often I'd find myself traveling with a colleague to meet with a client. For me, spending time in a car or a taxi with someone I knew professionally was easier to do than it was with a stranger, but I still felt uncomfortable. Silence wasn't an option in my mind. This was until I was on my way to a meeting with John, my boss at that time. We'd been working together for several months; however, we were rarely sitting together in a car. We had a good working relationship, but I was still learning, and I felt I needed to asked questions. After some casual banter John politely suggested we take a little time in silence. It shocked me somewhat and I spent the rest of the journey wondering why. At the time, I thought that I must have been annoying him. It didn't occur to me that John may have had things he wanted to think about, perhaps completely unrelated to the client we were about to meet. I should have asked why he suggested it, because it took another few years before I understood how silence worked.

They say, "silence is golden." In my coaching work, it's one of those "tools" I use when I need to create space for myself and my client. It's one of the toughest skills to master, especially when you are being paid to sit across from someone and ask them effective questions to help them on their journey. Silence creates space for all involved in a conversation. It creates the space for us to process what we've just heard. It creates space to find new ideas and be creative. It's been awkward in many places because my conditioning suggested there was something wrong if you had nothing intelligent to say.

The most profound experience I have had with respect to silence occurred when I was the client in a formal setting. My counterpart was very skilled in the use of silence. He invited me to take some time before we got started on the 60-minute session. He said nothing more. We'd worked together on stuff for a few years and I knew what he was doing. That didn't make it any easier. Initially, my mind was preoccupied with the concern that I didn't have anything relevant to share. As the minutes ticked away, and my mind let go I went to a completely new place. I was conscious that I could share when I was ready. I was also aware that I didn't need to. I was also aware that I had to stay there. I was paying for it after all and should aim to get my money's worth. My mind fought the silence. It raced around trying to find something to share. Eventually I obtained some calm and let go of the idea that I had to share something. Once I did that, I became more aware of my thoughts. I found I could test each thought as it arrived. I was able to ask myself if there was anything about that thought, that concern or issue, that I needed to share. The answer I kept getting back was "no." The sense of release was overwhelming. Being able to explore each thought without the burden of the need to share was like having a long shower. I felt released of everything my mind was shouldering. I felt free of my worries and concerns. The managed silence over that 60-minute session provided me with the space to truly assess what was important to me right at that moment.

It is all there between the words

My journey into greater self-awareness coincided with learning how to communicate better. However, that didn't translate into engaging more with the person next to me on planes, trains, and buses. There were three aspects that I began to appreciate. The first was how important silence is, even in well-established relationships. Secondly, I started to appreciate the situation wasn't just about me—there was at least one other person there to consider. And, finally, I realized that engagement is still a choice. Sometimes I don't want to engage and that is perfectly fine.

When I suggest silence is good for relationships, I am not referring to "the silent treatment." Premeditated disengagement, when not being bullied or abused, is also a form of abuse. Purposefully refusing to acknowledge an approach or intentionally holding back, is not healthy for anyone involved. Holding things back and ignoring others chews us up inside. It hurts the other parties and it is a potentially damaging behavior for our loved ones to have to witness.

For silence to work within relationships, of any kind, there needs to be a similar understanding of "the gap." The gap is the amount of time we leave between sentences. When we share something or tell a story, we do so with multiple sentences. We use small gaps to break the sentences and a long gap when we are finished. Those short gaps between sentences create both opportunities and discomfort. If the person listening typically talks faster and uses a smaller gap, they can frustrate the person talking because they "butt in" before the line of thought is finished. Equally, when the person with the smaller gap is talking, they can get frustrated with what they perceive as lack of engagement.

This is because they finish their story and expect a response but don't get one, so they feel they need to add more. This may not be the case, as the other person might be simply thinking they haven't finished and are only pausing between sentences. I find I have a slightly longer gap than most (that shortens as I drink alcohol), which can be very annoying to anyone sober around me. Healthy engagement, therefore, involves being clear when my gap is being used inappropriately. Equally, I might need to shorten or lengthen my gap to accommodate people who don't get it. Either way, I need to know my own gap, so I have a better chance of being true to myself when communicating with others.

A sign of a healthy relationship is when all parties understand the needs relating to silence. When there is a good understanding of what is normal, communication thrives, even when nothing is being said. Those with a strong bond can sit for long periods of time in complete silence and feel totally at ease, even when facing each other.

Getting beyond myself helps when sitting next to someone I don't know. There are times when I want to enjoy my own thoughts. Then there are times when I'd love to engage and learn something. However, it isn't clear from the offset which is the case and that can cause stress with those that feel it's rude not to speak. I find the easiest way to behave is to just smile and let the rest unfold. I do it immediately after I sit down or just as the other person does. I find the smile reduces my anxiety and theirs. The smile is an invitation, but it doesn't provide a commitment. If I get a response that suggests an interest in conversation but not the confidence to start (i.e., I get a smile back), I simply add "Hello" or "Hi." The conversation may or may not start. That's perfectly fine with me because I tried. Trying relieves any guilt I may have carried in the past. However, just smiling wasn't easy to do because of the fear of getting caught in a boring or annoying conversation. The breakthrough came for me when I realized the key to starting confidently, was to have a method to get out. This is needed if I find myself in a place where I don't really want to engage, or I find I am not interested in what they want to share. The first method is simply to use silence. Saying nothing for a time often works. If that fails, I have another strategy. I start by acknowledging them, with something like "that was really interesting, thank you for sharing." I make sure I use past tense. Then, before they can respond, I add something like, "Do you mind if I do some reading?" or "Do you mind if I catch up on some sleep?" It doesn't always work, but it's better than feeling guilty for hours, or days later.

Feeling worthy

The real lessons in my journey aren't always obvious. Uncovering something is only the starting place. It often takes other interrelated events for the real meaning to be clear. Choosing not to speak to the person next to me, is about appreciating how to use silence, but it's also about something deeper. The fact is that I don't need to be friends with everyone, and I don't need others to like me. I can feel worthy without them liking me. Learning about silence and how to use it effectively showed me what I was really doing. I was caught up with trying to befriend everyone and be liked by everyone. It is clear to me now that it isn't as important as I believed it to be. How I feel about me is far more important. Liking myself is a bigger priority. This appreciation gave these experiences a new perspective. I don't have to speak to the person next to me, however I can choose to.

Chapter 6: Return the borrowed beliefs

Without question

We have all been there, in a new place and being asked "What do you do?" It's a strange sort of a question really. While we know it means "What kind of work do you do?" it can be a great indication of how authentic our behavior is. For example, if I answered "nurse" or "engineer" or "work for ABC technology company," then I am not really describing "what I do." A better response might be "I nurse people back to full health," or "I build bridges," or "I help make smart phones." These responses do help communicate something more about what I do, but it's still not fully realizing the potential of the question. I can get more from my relationships by being more open and more specific. For example, I could have said, "I use my knowledge and empathetic nature to assist people in recovery so that they move back quickly to having rich and productive lives." Or "I bring creativity and ingenuity to building bridges for roadways so that people and goods can move across our country more efficiently," or "I use my attention to detail and dependability to help build devices which make the world a smaller place." It's unlikely that anyone would use these latter responses in a first meeting with a stranger, but it begs the question as to why I filter and simplify how I communicate details about myself.

Picture a young man in the kitchen. He is cooking up a storm preparing the family dinner. He has the leg of lamb there in front of him. His father peers over his shoulder and says, "Make sure you chop off the end of the leg before you stick it into the oven." He turns to his dad and says, "What would I do that for?" Dad replies, "Because that is how you cook a leg of lamb." The young man isn't satisfied and questions him saying, "But why? How do you know?" Dad is getting annoyed now and responds with, "Well, because my mum told me that was the way to do it." The young man turns around and calls out, "Hey Gran, what's the story with cooking a leg of lamb?" Gran comes over and says, "Well Ben, what I do is I chop off the end of the leg before I put it in the oven." Ben replies, "But how do you know that is how to cook a leg of lamb?" Gran responds with, "Because that is how my mother always did it." So, Ben heads into the lounge and sits down on the sofa. "Nanna?" he says. Nanna replies, "What's up dear?" Ben asks, "Dad and your daughter tell me that to cook a leg of lamb I need to cut off the end of the leg first." Nanna grins, leans in and shares, "Well, dear, when I was your age, we were very poor, we lived in a small house and had a small oven. So, in order to fit the leg into the oven, I'd have to cut off the end."

Borrowed Beliefs are beliefs that I adopt without question. I adopt them without understanding the assumptions and context on which they were formed. They obscure my options and therefore limit my choices. They can also become the basis on which I hide from my responsibilities.

Beliefs

Beliefs drive our behaviors, consciously, and unconsciously. We use beliefs to evaluate our experiences. Also, in a sense, beliefs encompass our goals in that goals represent the desired future state of something that we value.

Beliefs address everything we do and experience. We have beliefs about what we eat, how we dress, and who we socialize with. Beliefs address the simplest of notions, like that of wearing matching socks. They address more complex notions of what we believe about how we greet people we've just met (i.e., should you shake hands firmly, go for one peck on the cheek or is it two, or even three, or what about a bear hug?)

Our beliefs drive how we work and play. For example, consider these questions:

1. What beliefs do you have relating to working away on your laptop, while in a meeting, or on a conference call?
2. What beliefs do you have about what are appropriate topics for conversations in the office, the home, or in the pub?
3. What beliefs do you have with respect to using phones while having dinner, minding the kids, or catching up with friends?

Beliefs also govern how we evaluate our experiences (i.e., we use them when we judge others on how they behave in a meeting or at the dinner table, or in passing in the hall, or not saying this or that).

The most interesting thing for me about beliefs, is that beliefs can be changed. In fact, they can be changed in an instant. All you need to do is revisit the assumptions or context from which the belief was formed.

For example, who thought football boots should be the same color? Or on a more serious note, what beliefs were shattered the day the two planes flew into the Twin Towers?

Beliefs can be changed, sometimes for the better, or sometimes not so much. As a youngster I learned that trying to catch the ball was important because when the ball hit my chest or head, it hurt. That belief served me for a period, then when my fingers got in the way trying to catch a hard cricket ball, I formed a new belief. I believed that I should not try to catch the ball, I should get out of its way instead. That belief didn't serve me as well because now I wasn't picked for the team.

License to compromise my potential

My learning about the "borrowed" nature of some beliefs took time and came at great cost. I discovered that being busy and making money, or just doing things for others, does not give me a license to compromise who I am and what I could be. Being busy is not a license to neglect my physical or mental health. It is not a license to compromise on what I do as a son, brother, mate, parent, friend, or colleague. Being busy doesn't give me the right to think, "How dare you say I'm cross, distracted, and never around! Everything I am doing, I'm doing for you!"

Making major compromises to my physical health, my mental health, and my relationships so I could stay busy and make money was very much part of how I approached my life. It is also, in a way, still part of my reality in that I see it around me. The fact that I was busy all the time and that I was creating enough means gave me a license to compromise the other aspects of my life. I saw it

43

as a license to neglect my physical wellbeing (i.e., not exercise as much as I should, overeat, eat poorly, drink too much, and get insufficient sleep). I saw it as a license to neglect my mental wellbeing (i.e., procrastinate about what I'm going to do, watch too much TV, read little, and generally give in to material rewards). This "license" also manifested in compromising my behavior (i.e., expecting more of those around me than I should, expecting to do less in other parts of my life, taking more graces than I should, breaking promises, and letting others down). All this resulted in me falling short of being the person I could be. In other words, I failed to live to my potential.

In his book *Talking to "Crazy"; How to Deal with the Irrational and Impossible People in your Life*, Mark Goulston explores the idea of being a martyr. This is the situation where people make a point of refusing to ask for help, even when they really need it. He explains that these people use guilt against others for not helping, even though they never give others enough opportunity to help. Mark explains that over time this behavior makes others feel annoyed and exasperated. I think this helps explain why believing that "busy-ness" as a license to compromise has the potential to really undo any good I might be trying to do. When making significant sacrifices for a good cause (i.e., my kids, a charity, or even those I work for), I risk starting to feel I have a right to demand more than I should from those I am trying to help.

Over the last 100 or so years, the generations that shaped my world had it tough. Those that went through the World Wars and the Great Depression had a sort of desperation for any kind of work. With technology advancement and robotics that may become a reality for future generations too. Anyway, I speculate that back then, there would have been a belief that any type of work, no matter what, was good, and a worthwhile pursuit. The kind of experiences at those times could also go part way to explaining the importance placed on paying the bills. Put in the context of people literally starving, together with the idea of any work is good work, could suggest that it is very important and worthwhile to be busy and paying the bills. However, I don't get the sense that my grandparent's generation compromised their wellbeing and who they were. I get the sense that they had balanced lives, even in the hardest of times.

I get the sense that respect for themselves and others was still very much a part of how they operated.

I'm not suggesting there is anything wrong with being busy or making money. We all must contribute and meet the needs of our commitments. The challenge, I propose, comes when the "being busy" part isn't productive. The challenge comes when I focus on the busy part instead of the productive part. That gets in the way of my being the best person I can be. In theory, "being busy" should equate to "being productive." In the past when most of us would have been growing things, making things, or moving things, being busy and being productive at the same time would be easily linked. Since we largely now work in the knowledge economy it has got a whole lot harder to equate busy-ness to productivity.

Peter Drucker wrote about the changing face of work in his 1967 book, *The Effective Executive*. He wrote that, "the executive is ... expected to get the right things done." While he was writing about managers and leaders, his predictions can now be applied to most roles. We now have far greater choice of how we spend our time and that choice directly impacts our ability to be productive. When I choose the "right things" (i.e., those aligned to who I want to be), I am productive. When I don't, I am not. Unfortunately, I can be just as busy working away on the things that take me further away from who I want to be. If I am not consistently choosing the right ways to use my time and energy, I may still get there in the end, but it's unlikely that I will have traveled the easiest or shortest path.

The opposite of busy-ness is having a "mind like water." This is how David Allen describes it in his 2001 book, revised in 2015, titled *Getting Things Done. The Art of Stress-free Productivity*. Mind like water isn't about having an empty mind and doing nothing but staring blankly out of the window all day. Mind like water is about being in a perpetual flow state. This is where we are 100% focused on what we are doing. We do that at the same time as being ready to effectively and efficiently handle any interruption or distraction. Eckhart Tolle says something similar in his work titled *The Power of Now*. Tolle suggests we should aim to be completely present in every moment, in everything we do, and in every interaction we have.

I no longer believe being busy and making money, or just being busy and doing things for others, gives me a license to compromise on who I am and what I could be. It is a harder and more challenging path. It is where, while being productive, I must also do my best to honor my mental and physical health. I must do my best at being a good son, brother, mate, parent, friend, coach, facilitator, business partner, community member, and citizen.

Limiting the choices

As I started to understand the idea of borrowed beliefs, I started to look at the beliefs I have around money, my career, my relationships, and what I wanted to become. I found that some of the beliefs weren't mine. For example, I had a belief that career success meant securing and staying in a permanent and pensionable job. I borrowed that belief from my parent's generation. I now have a new belief focused on a career path that makes the optimal use of my highest point of contribution. This is also more realistic given the economic climate and changes in how we employ and manage work.

I borrow beliefs from all sorts of places: my family, my peers, my work culture, my community, and from, of course, media.

Beliefs are very important. To perform at my best, I need to accept that some beliefs will serve me, some will not, and some will be neutral. The key thing is that I just need to make sure the beliefs I have are my own, formed on my own values and strengths, and not borrowed from someone or somewhere else.

I have found that a borrowed belief can obscure the options I allow myself to see. It obscures options that may be aligned to my strengths and my value system. This is because the borrowed belief is based on someone else's strengths and value system. By questioning the assumptions and context of a borrowed belief, I have found that I see other options which are more aligned to my value system. I also see what will take better advantage of what I do well.

46

As well as obscuring options, the danger I've found with borrowed beliefs is that they have a certain comfort. I found they have comfort because I can distance myself from the responsibility of the outcomes of the behaviors and experiences resulting from the belief. Somehow, I found I could numb myself to the consequences of any associated actions. This has significant ramifications in all kinds of situations, from personal to professional.

A key turning point for me was learning to give borrowed beliefs back. Borrowed beliefs can be hard to find because their impact can be subtle. This is unlike the obvious beliefs that don't serve me. Beliefs that don't serve me result in behaviors that don't help me feel good about myself, don't build confidence, don't create enjoyment, don't create value, and don't have a positive impact on the world around me. The process of uncovering borrowed beliefs involves building a deeper awareness of my strengths and values. I then use that awareness to question my behaviors and reactions. In doing so I uncover beliefs that are obscuring options. I also see what is providing me with the excuse to hide from the consequences of my actions.

Change is simple?

Change is not hard. Putting aside pride on the other hand, is. Resisting change is where I find it hard to accept there might be a better way to do something. It is where I find it hard to accept that what I believe is wrong. Change is hard when I let pride get in the way of my seeing another and perhaps better way to do something.

Change is simply the process of taking a new belief and using it instead of an old one.

Time after time, I have found that my certainty about how best to do something is suddenly unfounded. This idea is true of all aspects of my life, be it how I manage relationships, my career, projects, and even how I manage things I need to do (i.e., to-do lists).

I found that I hide behind the beliefs. I have found that when something isn't the way I want it, I stick to what I know even though I know it causes me other problems. I use the excuse of "change is hard" or "people don't change," or "you can't teach an old dog new tricks." This attitude simply gets in the way of my being the person I want to be. The simple fact of the matter is that what makes us humans vastly different than all the other creatures we share this planet with, is that we change. We find better ways of doing things all the time.

Along the way, I learned that the process of enabling this type of change is easier than I originally thought:

1. When I find myself disappointed with something I am doing or I perceive others are doing to me, I ask myself "What do I believe to be important about this?" and I write these down.
2. Then for each thing I have written down, I ask myself "What is important about this belief? What does it give me? Where does it put me? Where is it used?" I then write these answers down too.
3. For each of the subsequent answers, I ask myself "What is important about this? What is the context of this? What am I assuming?"
4. If I am unsure, I check my memory for other times I have applied the same sort of logic and look for anything else related to assumptions and context.
5. One of two things typically happen next. Either I find that I have borrowed this belief, or I no longer value the reasons on which the belief was based.

In all cases I either find a better way or find that I am now willing to search for one. Pride is still a stumbling block, but once I have clarified the reasons behind what I believe, I find it much easier to forgive myself and move on. Don't get me wrong, I don't have all the answers and I haven't got it all right, but I am willing to look for better ways.

Uncovering borrowed beliefs doesn't solve all my problems. However, working from a set of beliefs that are my own does make it that little bit easier to find the path that is truly of my own choosing.

Chapter 7: Show your cards

Say or do it now

It is easier to clean up sooner than later, so say it or do it now. Small breaks are easier to repair than big ones. Admitting something after the fact takes a lot more effort than disclosure ahead of time. Holding onto concerns or suggestions drains my psyche. The distraction caused in the short term by holding things inside might be enough to take me off the rails and away from my true path. The longer I divert off course, the harder it will be to get back on track. That's not necessarily a bad thing. Often the shortest path isn't the most scenic. However, I am shifting away from my authentic self when I hold back on what I think or feel in a given moment.

The Doorstep concept

While the Doorstep concept didn't sit well with me, I accepted it for a large part of my adult life, and the damage to my mental health was significant.

The Doorstep concept is the idea that I present a rosy picture of myself from the doorstep outwards. The concept is prevalent in many forms of social media. I'm staying with the Doorstep as the metaphor because it exists with or without social media. The idea here is that the doorstep is as far as most people get (i.e., I stand at my doorstep talking to visitors and don't invite them in, or I interact with others outside the home but never invite them over). This behavior is used in communities, churches, social circles, sports clubs, workplaces, and just about everywhere else. While this is a real physical behavior in many cultures, it also applies to the filters people put up to project themselves largely, I believe, because of insecurities. The Doorstep behavior is evident when I hide my fears and real concerns, when I falsely portray myself as being happy, having a great relationship with my partner and my kids. It is when I give the impression that I am part of a wonderful workplace or engaging social circle, when I am not. It is when I present a balanced and calm demeanor, when I am really burning inside. It is where I only show the rose-colored view. It is where I project this image to everyone outside, yet when the doors are closed, things are different. I am withdrawn, angry, abrupt, unfocused, prone to shouting and yelling at loved ones, and susceptible to abusing myself (i.e., with drugs, alcohol, and comfort foods).

Growing up, in college, and in my early years of working, I was blessed in that I was able to experience the joy of connection and openness, and sometimes pain. I wasn't fully transparent, as I didn't have a detailed enough image of who I was, but I didn't really have to present to be much more than what you saw. As my environment changed and I adopted new surrounds and cultures, the Doorstep concept became part of my existence. I got caught up in an environment that focused on the material aspects and working every moment to have the nice clothes and big house with all the fine things. I also got caught up going to great efforts to appear to others that everything was great, and nothing could be better. When I allowed the Doorstep concept to rule my behaviors, I failed to appreciate the damage I was doing to myself and those living around me. I failed to see the impact with this Jekyll and Hyde approach to behaviors.

Not starting from here

"There is no map. Pioneers have to imagine the way, not read it." – David Hieatt

Where do I start from, when my education systems, my communities, and my workplaces only pretend to promote original and innovative thinking? Finding push-back has been my typical experience when sharing something that I felt was new and exciting. It wasn't uncommon to be asked where I got the idea from. I'd be asked who researched it, or who wrote about it. I'd be asked about my credentials for having this thought. To have an original thought I was expected to have already written dozens of academic papers, toured fifty countries, spent ten years as a prisoner of war, or led an organization of 50,000 employees. It felt like because my life was "normal," I couldn't possibly have anything original to add to the human experience. Those that haven't experienced some degree of this form of discrimination are simply lucky, or have never tried.

While writing this book and looking for a literary agent and publisher, I was often asked what books I have written already. Go figure. To publish I must have already published. It is further evidence of the crazy conditions of this modern world where the call for original thought, innovation, and creativity is largely just lip-service.

Trying to share something new and exciting takes courage. Unfortunately, that courage gets whittled away if you get knocked back often enough. The courage gets replaced with a feeling of guilt that you haven't achieved enough to justify these crazy original thoughts you have.

So, where do I start? Well the only place to start is right here—the very spot I find myself in at any given moment. Adopting this approach doesn't suddenly open doors or move mountains, however worrying about where to start will certainly delay me from finding that one open door or clearer path.

Taking risks

With clarity on where to start, risks need to be taken. There is a philosophy that says hold your cards until you need to show them. It's based on the idea that if I have good cards, I should only show them at the right time to ensure I will win! I get that, however, when it comes to the cards that show what I am good at, I need to stop hiding them. There is little to lose in being myself. I need to share what I do well and be authentic about it. It is hard enough for me to truly know what I am good at. It's therefore unrealistic to expect others to know. One of the dreaded questions in job interviews was "What are you good at?" My conditioning told me I should not boast. I see it all around me, this idea of not owning what I am good at and not speaking openly about it. So I avoided looking at who I was and what I was good at. Instead, my interactions became a guessing game of what I thought they wanted to know. That didn't serve me well. It either annoyed the interviewers or put me in a role that didn't leverage my natural abilities.

When I hide my true self, I must spend lots of energy managing the lie others adopt about me. That lie often results in letting others down. If I portray that I am Mr Fabulous, others will expect that of me. It is inevitable then that I end up making apologies. Every time I use an apology, I erode the trust others have in me, and that I have in myself. I've often wondered what the phrase "I apologize" says about me when it's connected to lies and half-truths. Perhaps those resulting from the Doorstep concept or holding my cards? What if someone was to turn it around and ask, "Are you remorseful?" And, "Is there forgiveness being looked for here?" Furthermore, my assumption is that I am letting someone down. Perhaps I am not. Perhaps the other party knows I am not what I say I am and therefore doesn't need an apology. Perhaps those words "I apologize" are more about admitting to myself that I am not who I portray. Perhaps apologizing just cements the damage I've done to them and myself. Clearly, there are techniques to avoid the apology (i.e., by saying "I'm getting back to you now and here it is …" and not providing any excuses). A better approach might be to stop getting in a position where there is a need to apologize.

Showing my cards is not the same as publicizing everything about myself. Unfortunately, the world isn't a sugar-coated marshmallow land. I must put things in perspective and the right context. Stuff like date of birth, passwords, and bank account details aren't typically for sharing. There are plenty of opportunists who will take what I share publicly and use it for their own gain. No, I need to "show" my cards to those that I trust, rather than "publish" my cards to every man and his dog.

It does take effort to overcome the conditioning that tells me to project a false version of myself, not to share original crazy thoughts and to never take risks. However, the rewards are worth it. It's much easier to be open and honest when there are fewer secrets. Life got easier when I stopped living in a shadow of guilt about what I do well. Life got easier when I had less to reconcile with. When the truth is out there, there is less to manage and control. There is more energy to focus on what I truly want from my journey.

PART 2:
BE A REALISTIC
OPTIMIST

Chapter 8: Take a spear!

Into the jungle

When you go into a jungle, take a spear! Hoping for the best but ignoring the dangers will only get me eaten. I must put myself in the neighborhood of danger on a regular basis, if I want to have a rich and engaging life. Never going into the jungle for fear of finding a sticky and uncomfortable end, holds me back from being my true self. However, that doesn't mean I can avoid every danger or pitfall armed solely with a positive attitude. This idea is drawn from William Whitecloud's book, *The Last Shaman*, which is a wonderfully entertaining story of self discovery.

During a trip to Nicosia, in Cyprus, I went running in the south part of the old walled city. It contains lots of narrow, winding streets, which were fun to explore as I ran. I got more and more confident as I dashed about the streets, the cars, and the people. And, I came unstuck. I forgot where I was. I stopped considering that I was in unfamiliar surrounds. As I went to run past a streetside coffee stand, a small dog dashed out and nipped me on the ankle. It shocked me and I wanted to kick it and defend myself, until I realized it was me that was in the wrong place. This small dog was the property of the stall owner. I was invading the dog's space. I ran in fast without any warning. The dog's reaction was defensive, protecting his owner. I had gone into the jungle with my eyes wide shut.

Clearly, I'm not referring to going into a real jungle. I haven't done that myself; perhaps one day I will. No, I'm referring to the jungle that is my daily life; working and playing. That jungle inevitably involves dealing with challenging situations, typically involving other people but also my own doubts and fears. I need to equip myself appropriately. As one of my favorite fictional characters, Lee Child's ex-military cop character Jack Reacher says, "Hope for the best, plan for the worst." Reacher faces all kinds of seemingly impossible situations. While his typical kit as he ventures around the US, involves no more than the clothes on his back, an expired passport, a bank card, and a toothbrush, he always pauses, assesses, and prepares for danger. At times that is simply a matter of sizing up his opponents and looking for their weaknesses. At other times, he enlists help from his network to gain access to the arsenal necessary to prevail. When I simultaneously access and plan while looking positively at who I am and what I want, I am being a Realistic Optimist.

Getting through it

A great example that illustrates the benefits of being a realistic optimist is the story of United States military vice admiral, James B Stockdale. His story is told in the business leadership book by Jim Collins titled *Good to Great: Why Some Companies Make the Leap... And Others Don't*. Stockdale's story is striking because he spent eight years held captive during the Vietnam War. And, not only did he survive when many others didn't, but he prevailed. He was not only an inspiration to his fellow prisoners, but he became an inspiration to many others when he got out of internment. He was tortured many times and really had no reason to believe he would survive the prison camp, to see his wife again. The key to his success was in how he pictured the outcome, but balanced it with pragmatism. In his words:

"I never doubted not only that I would get out, but also that I would prevail in the end and turn the experience into the defining event of my life, which, in retrospect, I would not trade."

It was obvious that the pessimistic would flounder, however he also noted that the purely optimistic failed as well.

"They were the ones who said, 'We're going to be out by Christmas.' And Christmas would come, and Christmas would go. Then they'd say, 'We're going to be out by Easter.' And Easter would come, and Easter would go. And then Thanksgiving, and then it would be Christmas again. And they died of a broken heart."

The pure optimists fail to appreciate the gravity of their situation and make allowances for it. To prevail, Stockdale had to simultaneously retain faith that he would prevail in the end, regardless of the difficulties, at the same time as confront the brutal truths of his reality.

Getting out of corners

Over time, I found the skills I needed to get myself out of corners. I found the skills I needed to move from the darkness to the light, which shouldn't have been a surprise to me, in truth, as I've always been very prepared. I learned about the importance of dutiful preparation from a young age in watching my father pack four kids, two adults, a dog, and luggage into a small sedan for summer holidays. That number of people, with accompanying gear, doesn't get into that small space by chance. It needs to be placed purposefully to make use of every available piece of space. And the funny thing is, I never felt squashed, even with bags and gear in the foot wells and stuffed all around us. That attention to detail meant we had everything we needed to fully enjoy our time at the beach and visiting relatives. Having the right material stuff was important but not as important as having the right stuff in my head. To fully engage in the experiences I put myself into, I needed to pack the right stuff.

My family love to share the story of a friend that joined them on a camping trip. Let's call him Dave. The trip was challenging because Dave brought a big trailer that was too heavy for the vehicles they had. The trailer was useful because it carried lots of stuff, was very functional, and made the trip much more enjoyable for them all. However, it was a pig to get out of the camp site and that diminished the experience. The learning for them was not to be afraid of using the trailer, which may reduce the enjoyment during the camping. Instead they arrived at the conclusion that they simply needed to bring a bigger and more powerful vehicle to pull it.

My personal story has been similar. Rather than look to avoid the situations that diminish my experience, I've looked to obtain better skills in managing things so I can maximize the potential of those situations.

Avoiding the bus

Another way to look at realistic optimism is that a pessimist won't cross the road, while an optimist will cross the road without awareness. The pessimist never gets anywhere, while the pure optimist is eventually going to end up under a bus. The Realistic Optimist crosses the road with awareness of the dangers and makes allowances for them (i.e., avoiding crossing in front of a bus).

Chapter 9: Choice without burden

To be authentic or not to be authentic. It's a choice. I've found the biggest challenge in making that choice is knowing when I am leaning toward being authentic, rather than further away from it. The challenge is that choices are often laden with burdens.

There is nothing wrong with me

The statement "There is nothing wrong with me," is both the truth and a naive mis-conception. Everyone has edges that could be a little smoother. Everyone has character strengths that need to be managed. Everyone has behaviors that don't serve them well. It's a fact of our human nature. However, the existence of flaws doesn't mean something is wrong. It's the opposite. To have flaws is normal. On the other hand, holding the belief that I am without flaws is naive. It's naive to think or say things like "I don't have any problems to work on," or "I don't need help with anything." It simply not true that I have no aspect to improve or learn about. There is always something I don't know or some experience I could learn from.

Suicide is not a trivial matter. It creates all kinds of hurt for all those involved. Unfortunately, the belief that "there is nothing wrong with me," in large portions of society, makes it harder to truly reach and help those on the edge. While openness is often actively promoted, support organizations trying to break down the misconceptions, have their work cut out for them. The work they do is harder than it should be because of those clinging to the notion of "it's them, not me." Ideas like "sadness is something you are born with," allows people to distance themselves. It is hard to learn of a father taking his life. It's totally frustrating and upsetting to hear those around him using phrases like "there were no signs of any illness" or "he appeared perfectly normal." It's that naive understanding of the flaws in human nature that prevents them from seeing it in others. They use statements like these to distance themselves from the tragedy because they can't rationalize the sadness and frustrations with their own circumstances.

When I share that I have used psychotherapy to help regain balance, I usually get awkward silence. I know the look and I know what's on the minds of those I share the information with. I know this, because I too once held limiting beliefs about counseling and psychotherapy. I too believed, "There is nothing wrong with me." I believed that intervention was a sign of sickness and weakness. I came to appreciate that we all, if we are honest, have sad times, and feelings of being totally against the wall with no reasonable alternative. I came to appreciate that it is normal to have flaws and to have concerns. Unfortunately, it is often easier to look for distraction to avoid thinking about it.

The attitude that it's everyone else and not me is limiting, and potentially very dangerous. When in safe circumstances, the attitude will just prevent me from learning new and wonderful things. It will simply hold me back from experiencing my full potential. However, if I get hold of some super-positive affirmations and buy into that way of thinking, the consequences can be fatal. Having the attitude that I am without fault and invincible at the same time is like walking into the mouth of a lion with my hands tied behind my back. I am totally exposed and unable to defend myself.

Juggling complexity

The idea of choice without burden came to my attention when I was coaching an experienced executive. We were working on the challenge of juggling complex layers of conflicting wants, needs, and commitments. The conflict is a burden. Firstly, I must carry the weight of where I find myself right now. This relates to the impact of my past choices. Secondly, I must carry the weight of the future. This relates to the burden of the choices I have before me now.

It's rare that a day goes by that I am not reminded of the burden of the choices I made in the past (i.e., the aspects in my world that I should continue to nurture or maintain, the obvious example being the emotional and financial support relating to my five wonderful children). Another example would be the bills that need to be paid to put food on the table and keep a roof over my head. Then of course, there are the commitments I have made to my family, my friends, my communities, my colleagues, and my customers, the job I took, the project I started, and the volunteering work I got involved in. All these choices in the past bring real conflicts of commitment to my present.

The burden from past decisions is optional. When I look negatively at these past choices, I feel like a victim of the situation; I try to find someone or something to blame. But when I look positively at the past choices, I see a different reality. I see the great things that I have done. I see what has taken place to bring me here. I see what has helped prepare the set of opportunities that lie before me. As an example, when I focus on the lack of personal time I got from the choice of having children or volunteering to fundraise for my community, I seek to blame. When I focus on the wonderful experiences, the friendship, the joy, and the learning opportunity I get from those same choices, I seek to embrace, and engage.

Comfortably numb

There are many who have seen success financially, have held power, have been super-fit, or devoted rafts of time to charities, but have then settled for something less when it comes to "being". They accept a "second" place when it comes to full engagement with everyone and everything around them. They choose to hide behind those aspects of their lives where they are succeeding and neglect the things that will really bring them meaning.

Life is challenging. I am continually confronted by things that don't go the way I hoped. I am continually confronted with the question of "do I give a damn?" I then face the choice of looking for new ways to progress or the choice of surrendering to avoidance. By avoidance I mean things like disengagement, overeating, inactivity, box sets, and computer games. I also mean the more committed forms of avoidance like alcohol, drugs, working long hours, and even fitness training at the expense of everything else. By surrendering, I am accepting the avoidance. Those that are lucky enough to have a good position, influence, money, power, and health, risk finding themselves being comfortably numb.

Being comfortably numb is where I waste my time and energy. Where I don't care enough about being the best I can be. I keep busy, bank the pay check, and then collect things to help maintain the comfort. I avoid confronting the things that will really bring meaning. I fear making any real changes, letting go of some of the comforts. I fear what I would have to face if I couldn't hide behind the comforting, but limiting, beliefs I have about myself.

Looking around

Maintaining a positive aspect when looking backward is not straightforward. When the challenges come hard and fast, it gets overwhelming. When I succumb to the overwhelm, I distance myself from those choices and look for someone or something to blame. I've employed numerous coping strategies over the years. I have used friends and family, self-help books, motivational speakers, coaches and mentors, counselors and psychotherapists. Each method has its place and each offer different benefits and drawbacks. Friends and family have helped me look at things I'm focused on in my immediate past. They provide a nice place to look for similar experiences and hopefully gain some insights. Self-help books and motivational speakers are a great way to see the types of experiences facing the wider community. They help me understand how they have managed those situations. Coaches and mentors help me take a different perspective on my experiences and bring me back to the present. They help me see how I will leverage past learning to move forward. Counselors and psychotherapists help me explore conditioning and its impact on how I perceive the outcomes of my choices. Each method needs to bring me to a place where I own my past choices, and in doing so, release the burden.

In looking forward, the burden comes from the complexity and volume of the options before us. Making choices with a cluttered mind is like trying to prepare a big dinner for family and friends in a kitchen already jammed full of dirty dishes. I have found there is no sense of burden when I take control, get clear in my head about what I want and focus on one thing at a time. In the absence of burden, I get more done, and have more time to explore what it really means to choose my own path.

The white space

The sense of relief that comes when there is no burden, creates space. It gives me the opportunity to explore more about who I am and what it all means.

When I choose actions or put myself in the way of experiences that are aligned with my true self, I am more inclined to feel enthusiastic and engaged, as well as have a better chance of being the person I want to be. A better understanding of who I am has helped me make better choices about where I put myself and what I do when I am there. It helps me focus on how to best use my precious time and energy.

I use the following model to help assess where my focus is as I look at the choices I have before me. The model has two questions. The first question is to ask myself if I see meaning and purpose in every action I take and every experience I have. In other words, are my experiences free of doubt or burden? The second question is to ask myself if I feel everything that I do and experience is an optimal use of my time and energy. In other words, am I always in a calm state and getting what I want done in the time I want it to get done? Putting yes and no against these two questions gives me a place in the model.

I have the tools I need; however, I could build better awareness of who I am.

Do I see meaning and purpose in every action I take and every experience I have?

I know who I am, and I have the tools I need.

NO   YES

Do I feel that everything I do, and experience is an optimal use of my time and energy?

YES

NO

My choices have me doing things the right way, but those things may not always be the right ones.

My choices have me doing the right things the right way.

My choices don't always have me doing the right thing and those things aren't always done the right way.

My choices have me doing the right things, but not always the right way.

I could build better awareness of who I am, and I could make use of more efficient ways to think and act.

I know who I am; however, I could make use of more efficient ways to think and act.

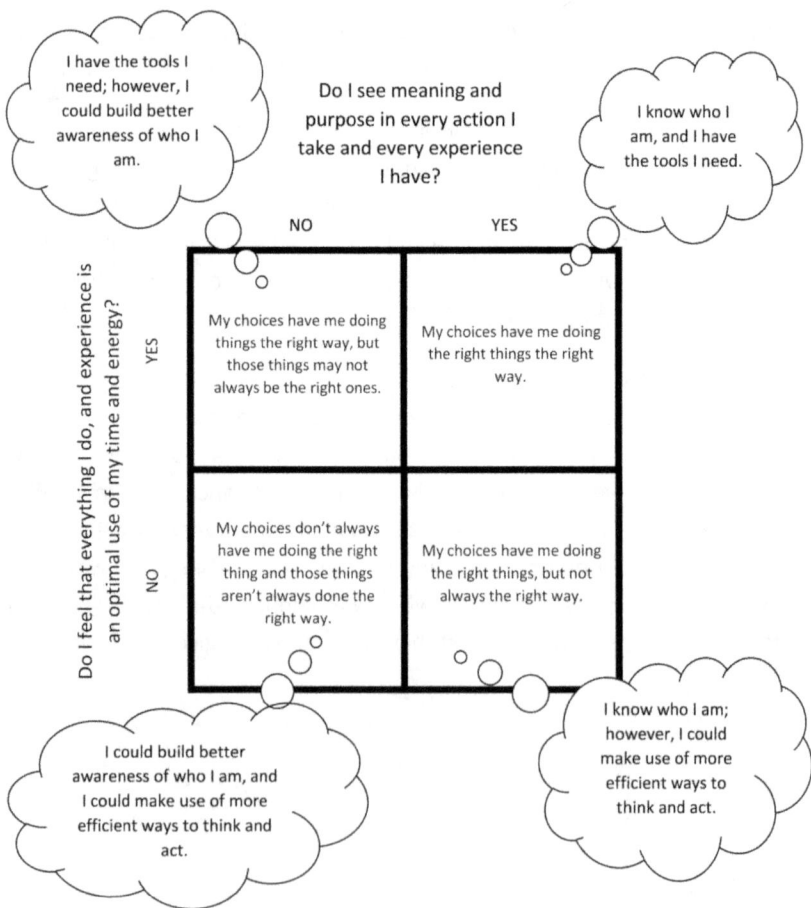

In the bottom-left corner, I am often finding myself doing things that I don't feel serve me. I find that doing these things is hard and exhausting. In the bottom-right corner, I feel good about the things that I am doing, but I am still exhausted and continually playing catch-up. In the top-left corner I am doing things well and maintaining a good level of energy, but I don't feel I am doing enough to get ahead or serve others well. In the top-right corner, I am in flow, maintaining energy, and doing wonderful things for myself and all those around me.

Where I am

Where I put myself and what I do when I am there, is directly related to my ability to make good choices. Putting myself in the right place has two extremes: the "suck it and see" and the "leave nothing to chance" approach.

When I use the first approach, "suck it and see," I don't get weighed down by what may or may not happen. I hope that I will be in the right place at the right time. I take the chance that I will be able to handle everything that comes at me. Using the game play analogy, I hope that I will be in the right place at the right time to catch the ball. I won't get bogged down by worrying what will happen when the ball comes in my direction. I won't spend time over thinking how I will catch it. I would congratulate myself on being able to spontaneously react as needed to make that great catch. In taking this approach I am assuming that I will have enough warning to see the ball and adjust my position. Unfortunately, when things get complex, this approach has the risk of having me run all over the place trying to catch everything. This approach also runs the risk of completely missing the play altogether (i.e., not even being aware that a ball went past because of all the energy and attention being given to catching the others). On the other hand, this approach is a lot of fun and, owing to the pace, can give the impression of being very productive.

The opposite approach leaves nothing to chance. I will spend lots of time and energy looking at everything that is going on and that is coming down the line. Using the game play analogy, I will systematically analyze every aspect of the field, the players and the stakes, in order to anticipate exactly where the balls will need catching. Then I will ensure that I, or someone else, is there to take the catch. Nothing gets through. In this approach, I am assuming that every ball must be caught. Unfortunately, as things get complex, this approach has the risk of my spending so much time in anticipating everything, that I never get onto the field of play.

Clearly, neither approach works in isolation. Both result in less than productive outcomes, wasted energy, and focus on too much of the wrong things. The balanced approach is simply about understanding the level of importance.

As someone from a project management background, I have had to train myself to spend less energy anticipating every play. I have had to learn to get onto the field more and in doing so put myself in a position to better understand what was important. Equally, I've had first-hand experience of the aftermath, the fallout. I've experienced those focused at the other end of the spectrum, in that they consider it possible to handle every piece of play on the field and catch every ball, without any organizing, or preparation.

Some plays will have a significant impact on the result and others won't. The difference between these minor and major plays is the level of importance. The analysis helps understand this, but it isn't the full solution. This is because the level of importance isn't always evident from the offset and only becomes clear once the play is underway. In other words, a lot of the time I need to be on the field catching balls to really see what is happening in the game. That said, I do need to have a sense of the direction and intensity of the play in advance so I can put myself in the general vicinity of where the balls will be landing.

There is one final piece in this line of thought. There are times when I need to abandon the game altogether. If I am provided with an opportunity that gets in the way of my plans, I need to choose. Consider what I should do if I have made plans for an early start. Perhaps I have made a personal commitment to get some exercise first thing in the morning before starting work. However, the sun is shining and it's a perfect opportunity to meet friends, have a meal by the water and enjoy some beer or wine. That has the potential to get in the way of my plans for tomorrow. I need to assess what is important.

In work and play, the level of importance is down to one thing—values. From the values come beliefs, and those beliefs drive behaviors and how I evaluate my experiences. So whether I lean toward the "suck it and see" or the "leave nothing to chance" approach, or face abandoning the play altogether, I still need to have a good understanding of what I see as important. We will explore values further in chapter thirteen.

The pause

In facing down the choices that drive my journey, there is one option I must consider, and often don't. No matter how many choices are before me, there is always the choice to pause. Pausing isn't the same as being comfortably numb or doing nothing. There is still engagement with choice in these scenarios. Continuing to process and consider the choices changes me and that changes my choices. Causality is in play (i.e., all that I think and do has an effect; things shift and change and so do my choices). Pausing simply implies I choose not to choose for a moment or two. Instead I listen. As we will explore further in chapter eighteen, when I choose to pause and listen, I access The Light. When I do that, I am creating the space for the answer to present itself to me.

Chapter 10: Perspective and absolutes

While The Light, the unseen force that seamlessly brings the right things together at the right time, flows around me, I must focus to stay within it. I like to imagine that I am always doing my best at any given moment to be my best self. However, that isn't realistic because everything is relative, and nothing is absolute.

Troughs and peaks

I operate with a relative perspective. I judge my situation and that of others based on my perspective. Let's look at how I might climb a mountain. If I was asked to judge my progress in the valley at the start of the climb, I might look up, see the peak, and give myself a goal. Perhaps I might say, "My goal is to climb halfway." Then as I progress, I might look up and see that I've climbed 50% of the way to the peak I saw in the valley, and then conclude "I am done." I might conclude I can rest and take comfort in the knowledge that I have achieved my goal. I could boast and celebrate this success. From my starting perspective this is reasonable. Those who were with me in the valley will congratulate me and give me reason to feel successful. But what if the peak I saw was only a lower ridge on the slopes of the mountain? The true nature of the task would have been obscured by my perspective in the valley. If I share my delight with someone who knows the true scale of the mountain, I will look foolish. It's unlikely I will get any recognition and that will be confusing for me.

Another way to look at perspective is to explore a rock. If I put myself in the eyes of the rock, sitting on the ground observing myself and my surrounds, I will see things moving past me, some fast, and some slow. I observe myself relative to these things. I see myself as stable, unmoving, whole, complete, and wanting for nothing. I could say I am at total ease with myself and my place. What if I were now to step outside the eyes of the rock. What if I was to inspect the rock at an atomic level. What would I see? Well, I would see atoms, and particles moving rapidly. I would see a seemingly chaotic environment of many separate entities, all racing around the place, in constant movement. Now, what if I was to try to explain that to the rock. What would the rock think if I told it that it wasn't solid, whole, and static inside? The rock would struggle to conceive this as true, simply because its perspective doesn't allow it.

From an early age I hated boating because I got seasick. I would start to get unsettled with the slightest movement of the boat. The imbalance across my senses was foreign and therefore unsettling. The stress would increase, and I would start to shut down. My stomach would start to turn, and I would feel physically weak. It was frightening. It was the worst feeling that I could ever imagine. If asked how I was feeling out of 1-10, I would have given it a zero, without any doubt. I got used to avoiding the onset of that feeling. I conditioned myself to recognize the early signs and hold myself back. However, something still drew me to the sea. I started to learn to sail in the calm confines of Sydney harbor. I would avoid being below deck and that pretty much kept things on an even keel. Eventually I joined a crew and was having such a brilliant time that I kept getting more involved. Before I knew it, I was on a 40ft racing boat on my way to Hobart in the middle of a storm. Avoiding going below deck was no longer an option. I got scared; the body didn't respond well to the pounding waves and the constant movement; and I got sick. I was sicker than I could have ever imagined. I kept doing my job, on deck, and off deck every 3 hours. I vomited on and off for 36 hours both above and below deck. Nothing stayed down. Not even water. I got to the point that there wasn't anything more to come up. Another 12 hours and I would have been in serious trouble. With the encouragement of some of the closest friends I have ever had, I started to take some water and then dry crackers. That helped me feel a little better. The glimmer of hope changed everything. I let go of my fear and I got well, almost instantly. I found myself in a state of euphoria. I couldn't believe how better I felt. For the first time after two years of sailing, I found I could come and go below deck as needed. Once I would dread going below, even when I was so tired that I could barely move. Now, I was actively looking for reasons to go below, even if just to make someone a cup of tea. People talk about getting sea legs, but I always thought that was exclusively physical conditioning. I now know it is also mental. I still feel odd below deck or in rough seas. My stomach feels odd and my mind doesn't like the confusing messages it receives. However I now have a new reference point, a new perspective. I know things can be much, much worse, and that knowledge helps me stay calm. With that knowledge and calmness, my body recovers, and the stress is avoided. I don't spiral into the abyss.

Embracing changes in perspective allows me to see progress and reassess my path. It also provides the opportunity to take another look at my priorities. When the mist clears and I see where I am, I can leverage it to build momentum. I can reset my milestones and drive on. Equally, when I look back down at the valley from the ridge, I see the valley in a new light. I can look at why I left the valley and consider the importance of what I am doing against that new perspective. Perhaps now that I am on the ridge, I realize it wasn't as exciting as I thought. I see what I valued about the valley. I can reframe that against why I am climbing the mountain.

While I have no choice in that I can't know what I don't know, I still need to be cautious not to frame every future moment and decision based on past perspectives or only what I see. I must be ready to reassess and rewrite my goals based on new perspectives as I move forward.

Grounding

Spending time with family and old friends provides the opportunity to remind myself of who I am and where I came from. Reuniting with family or friends that I don't see regularly enables me to experience my previous self. This is useful and dangerous. The beliefs and behaviors that served me growing up may not serve me now. Equally, I can benefit from being reminded of some aspects that might be better than what I now believe and how I currently behave. Those that I don't see very often will still hold the old version of me, as I of them. I fall back into language and manners that I used in their company, which is largely a good thing. It's comforting and enriching. It's the reason so many of us gather for yearly holiday celebrations.

It is during these grounding gatherings that I am reminded of two hard facts of life.

Firstly, my children will eventually grow up and leave me. It is important, therefore, that I maintain my personal existence, my personal space, my friendships, and my intimate relationship. Putting everything into my kids isn't the best for them and it isn't for me either. They become too dependent on me and will struggle in life and will still leave, eventually (unless of course they never leave me, which might be even worse).

Secondly, I will get old, and some of those I care about will die before me. Family and friends may relocate and lose touch with me. I will change jobs and lose contact with colleagues. I will change over time and may no longer relate to those people already in my life. Some of those I hold dear will change over time and no longer want to be around me. And, most importantly, when I break off a long-term relationship, some of my friends may take sides. The learning, then, is to make friends where I can and don't get over reliant on any one circle (i.e., losing touch with my own friends and socializing only with my mate's friends is a disaster waiting to happen). It not only puts me at risk of being alone at some point, it is an awful burden to put on my mate. Spreading the risk is a topic that we will explore further in chapter fifteen.

I have been lucky that I've had a close relationship with my siblings and parents. Living on the other side of the planet means there isn't a lot of time spent together. When it does happen, it is rich, and rewarding. However, the time together does need to be managed as it has the potential for derailment. This is because the aspect that makes this time so enjoyable is the same aspect that might get in the way of growth. That aspect is nostalgia. For me, family time is enjoyable because everyone feels safe and unburdened with pretense. It's a place where things are said because we care about each other. It's a place where honesty and good intention is assumed. It is a place where we can expect to be put back in our box if we behave badly, like a time when I snapped at my sister while helping her with her laptop. The look I got from her was a big reminder of how things could go horribly wrong for me if I kept that tone. It is like that because that is how it was when we were all kids. Dropping back into family or old friend comfort zones has its downsides. Not only do I risk behaving in my old limiting manner, but those around me may also treat me as they have always known me. This has two problems. Firstly, any changes

I've made to better myself might get suddenly undone, like giving up smoking, or cutting back on drinking, or taking up exercise. And secondly, anything new or different may not be tolerated or accepted. Like contrary belief systems or different approaches to managing complexity. Appreciating this is key to experiencing the good aspects of time with loved ones.

Absolutely not, but sometimes

Perspective both enables and inhibits my progress. What I believe of the world and my place in it depends on several factors, not just what I see for myself. I also must consider what others see. I take viewpoints from all those around me and from what I experience. Some of what I experience is designed to manipulate me, like advertising. From the perspective I create measures and I use them to assess my place and progress. The key is to create the best measures for me, not others. When the measures are derived from someone else's perspective I run the risk of derailing. I run the risk of progressing toward someone else's version of what is good for me, not my own. The tell-tale signs, as explored in chapter four and chapter six, involve the use of absolutes. Using terms like "only," "never" or "always" indicate a belief that may not be derived from my own perspective. Some examples include: "I always go to the gym on Mondays and Wednesday," "I only eat cake on special occasions," "I never drink mid- week," "I always call my parents on Sundays," "I never think bad of anyone," and "I only watch TV for an hour a day." Anything expressed in an absolute is not true. There is only one absolute fact and that is that there are no absolutes in truth, only varying degrees of perspective. That is funny, right?

Sometimes I eat fried chicken and sometimes I don't. By removing the absolute (i.e., "I don't eat fried chicken"), I remove the guilt I suffer when I do eat fried chicken. This also applies to other vices, like drinking alcohol, or smoking or playing computer games. It becomes a better way of seeing what works. Further examples include, "sometimes I exercise and sometimes I don't," "sometimes I eat well and sometimes I don't," and "sometimes I go to the gym, sometimes I don't." Another subtle variation of this theme is the contradiction. For example, I could also use "I never eat fried chicken, apart from when I do," or "I always go to the gym daily, apart from when I don't." It still works.

Living with absolutes increases the potential for over-confidence as well as hiding in the comforts. I orientate myself toward fear and bring on unnecessary stress. All that holds me back. It assumes I am already at the end of the line. It assumes I have already reached the top of the mountain. It assumes I have already reached my potential.

Avoiding absolutes opens me up to the potential for learning. When I leave a space for being wrong, I have a better chance of seeing the new perspective. When I remove the need to always or never do something or not do something, I appreciate the sunshine, and brightness as well as the mist, the clouds, and the gloom. I see it all as potential for a new perspective.

Perspective risk

While flawed, I know my perspective is still fundamental to making decisions. To choose my own path, I need to make decisions and those must be made with some level of certainty. Even when I am prepared for that certainty to be undone, I still must make decisions. The trick is to test my perspective so that the level of trust is enough. That process is straightforward. I simply need to test my assumptions and look for gaps.

The process I use is as follows: First, I write down everything I know about where I am, how I feel, what I see, and whatever else I think will be true when I reach my goal. The list from our earlier mountain climbing story might look something like this:

I am here, with my two feet planted in the valley.

There are trees and rivers here.

There will be a wonderful view from the top of the mountain.

I can see only one way out of this valley.

I can see the top of the mountain, up there beyond the tree line.

I will feel brilliant at the top of the mountain.

I will see the whole valley from up there.

I have all that I need to get started.

I will have more options (i.e., paths to take), from the top of the mountain.

I can see the path I must take, from here to there.

The next step is to get help or use a very critical eye and review the list. I look for things I don't really know for certain. There are lots of examples in this list (i.e., "only one way out of this valley," "I can see the top of the mountain" and "I will have more options"). At this point I might find some other things to add to the list, like "I don't know what it is like being on top of the mountain I see before me" and "I don't know if the paths I see from the top of the mountain will be for me." From there, if anything is obviously wrong, I might rethink the plan. Otherwise, I'll set forth, bringing the list with me. Along the way, I'll take moments to reflect on this list again. I will check for things that are new, things that were wrong, and things that are still true.

When I manage it, instead of my perspective being a crutch or something to blame, it becomes a platform to learn and grow from.

Chapter 11: Fail well

Success driven

My upbringing, my education, and my workplaces all fell short of preparing me for failure. I was taught to aim for the good grades, to be a great sports person, to win the competition, to get that top job, and to get that promotion. The focus was on how I achieve success. While there isn't anything wrong with reaching the top, it's lifting myself up when I hit the bottom that troubles me. I wasn't taught how to use failure properly, to learn from it, to grow stronger from it, to become more resilient. This lacking in the skills needed to cope with life's challenges had me driving my existence to a dark place. It's far too complex to suggest the failing rests in any single place. As educators, as parents, as colleagues and friends, everyone shoulders that responsibility. They all have a role to play in helping each other understand failure. In doing so they can extract the learning and become stronger.

Imagine a world where people did what they say by when they said they'd do it, without needing to be reminded. Imagine a world where people actively renegotiated their commitments sufficiently ahead of time rather than being reminded of them when they'd already failed to deliver on them. Imagine a world where there was not a need to make allowances for those that rarely deliver on what they promise. I have often wondered what that world would be like. I wonder how much less mental energy the world would need. I wonder what things the world could accomplish. Then, I reflect, and think that perhaps that world would be too perfect, too contrived, and too easy. After all, it is the bumps, and wobbles in our journey that create the best opportunities for learning and growth.

Embracing the wobble

I may feel aligned. I may feel I have clarity. I may have confidence in the effectiveness and efficiency of my structures and systems. I may feel on top of my exercise, eating, sleeping, relationships, and career. No matter how good things are going, I always experience wobbles.

Watch a professional sports person performing and you may notice they are constantly correcting. Watch someone that is good with a skateboard and the same things happen. You may even know the feeling. At one moment I am cruising: the wind is in my hair, I am looking good, I am feeling good. Life is good. It couldn't be better. However, I am moving and by moving I am subject to constantly changing conditions: a stone, a break in the pavement, a gust of wind, something catching my eye, a distracting thought. Whatever it is, it will cause a wobble. What happens next is all too common. I don't become aware of the change in the conditions until it's too late. I over correct and end up on my arse. What's worse is that the faster I go the harder it is to correct the wobble and the harder the fall. Life is just like that.

The skateboard wobble image resonates with me. Growing up I was insanely jealous of my brother and my cousin. They mastered the skateboard, when I could not. I feared the wobble and avoided it. I didn't embrace the learning potential. That fear projected into my life as a recurring theme.

The trick is to get used to the wobble. Get used to sensing it coming on. Get practice at correcting and adjusting. Get to know how to change direction, balance, and even speed. And most importantly, get used to taking falls. I can't always catch the wobble. Sometimes I am going to take a fall. However, a fall is a good thing. It helps me see where my boundaries are at now. Over time, I find I can pick up more speed, take more risks. The wobbles become less frequent and I get better at handling them when they do occur, even at speed.

I apply this to life. I use this idea to get better at noticing and then correcting. I have learned to learn from the wobbles.

Built in know-how

Relationships that last do so because the know-how to get out of trouble is built in. The skills to navigate through and out of stormy waters is part and parcel of the deal. As explored in chapter three, things don't go so well when there is insufficient investment in preparation and maintenance in the foundations of a relationship. Things fail when I lack the knowledge of how to leverage the downturns to create upward momentum.

My personal experience of marriage is a perfect example of how things turn ugly when the know-how to sail through troubled waters is lacking. After many years and five children, my first marriage was dissolved. It wasn't a sudden end, it crumbled to pieces over time. While plenty of effort was made to keep things together, the relationship turned into a battle zone. It didn't end amicably.

Explaining what went wrong isn't easy because there weren't any of the classical hurdles like infidelity. The most simplistic assessment would say that we weren't compatible. It could be said that our paths intersected for a time, but there wasn't really a joining of our journeys: that we are too different, and our values and ideas of what we wanted in life were just too diverse. However, the truth is more complex. We got way down the track, but still failed to see it through. The demise after such a long period can't be simply explained through incompatibility. That reasoning doesn't account for all the wonderful times.

When we met, I was in an overly optimistic place. I was highly motivated. I felt unstoppable. I felt I could achieve anything just with a positive attitude and affirmations. My state of mind was intoxicating and we both got caught up in the reality I had romanticized. However, my version of the future and the plan I had for what I thought was important, was flawed in lots of ways. It resulted in both our truths being compromised. Neither of us existed as our authentic selves. This produced some great times and interesting experiences, and it was very productive in terms of creating a family, but it wasn't based on authenticity and eventually it all unraveled, spectacularly. Over time, things were realigned with our own truer selves, and when that happened there wasn't much left to be the basis of a relationship. It was too late by the time this reality was evident.

There were also other major factors working against us. Trying to parent at the best of times is challenging, but with a flawed foundation in the relationship it is nearly impossible. Being a parent on top of all the other financial and non-financial commitments puts serious demands on our focus and energy. With what precious time is left, watching mindless box sets, reality TV, or films becomes a far more attractive proposition than sharing a meal, a glass of wine, some banter, or anything close to intimacy. There is absolutely no time left for repair. Without the preparation and ongoing investment, a marriage becomes a largely repetitive and uninspiring existence. While the growing process brought about more truth, it also caused conflict. The marriage failed because the conflict wasn't managed well. We simply lacked the foundations in our relationship to turn mistakes and challenges into lessons. There was insufficient commitment to failing well. Learning must be at the center, and it wasn't.

Reading the signposts

Infidelity isn't the cause of broken relationships. Being unfaithful is simply the clearest sign that a relationship is broken. Infidelity is a break in the contract of the relationship, pure, and simple. It implies that there was a contract in the first place. When two people fail to invest properly in how their relationship is built and maintained, it creates cracks. Over time the cracks widen. Those cracks create opportunities and the result can be cheating. That doesn't mean it's inevitable. Cracks can exist for years in relationships with no infidelity. Equally, relationships end all the time with no cheating.

When the commitment is strong, even with the cracks, opportunities don't get capitalized on. Being someone who has a strong need to honor my commitments and associated values, I was bound to the vows I made before my friends and family. Even with years of travel, meeting lots of wonderful people, and the many lonely nights, that commitment was kept. Even as the marriage broke down and when the anger and frustration seemed never ending, I still held true. Some tell me now, looking back, that my devotion was in vain, however the learning, and resulting resilience I built from the experience, has paid me back tenfold.

When things get off the rails and cheating does occur, the opportunity for learning can be diminished if either person looks to blame the demise of the relationship on the infidelity. The learning potential is vastly improved if both see the infidelity as an indicator that the contract has been broken. The key is to look for sources, not causes. For the person who strayed, the act allows them to look at themselves and explore what they felt before and during the experience. Those feelings pave the way to insight. Exploration of this type provides the place to understand expectations and needs. The exploration can help understand what needs weren't being met. For the person left blindsided by infidelity, they can be honest with themselves, and look at how they behaved within the relationship. This too provides the path to insight. They can look at their expectations and needs, as well as the expectations and needs of their partner, and explore what wasn't being met. The learning that results builds their own skills in how they engage with others, and hopefully can be the basis of stronger and more fruitful relationships.

The risks associated with failure to understand the learning potential of infidelity, has impact over the longer term. Instead of focusing in to the relationship, those faced with this challenge can choose to focus outside, looking for ways to reduce or eliminate the opportunity for infidelity. This transfers into any future relationship, where they reduce their experience and the potential, through what they do to themselves and the other person. They will feel scared when their partner goes out or travels. They will fear that since they can't see what their partner is doing, the opportunities for infidelity will be ripe, and fear the negative outcomes, no matter how unfounded. Equally, they will restrict how they engage with others for fear that they might not be able to control themselves. They will focus on the infidelity rather than their own relationship. Instead of investing in behaviors that build trust, they invest in behaviors that create cracks.

Infidelity is a sure sign that something is broken and points to a learning opportunity. Equally, the learning opportunity exists in stale relationships— those where there isn't any cheating, yet. The signs are there in these relationships long before things get scary. The opportunity always exists to eat some humble pie and take a hard look at what they are doing in all aspects of their experience. Relationships of all kinds are no exception. Chapter fifteen takes a deeper look at social needs, which will be helpful to anyone wanting more from their relationships.

The right mindset

"Success is stumbling from failure to failure with no loss of enthusiasm." – Winston Churchill

"Only those who dare to fail greatly can ever achieve greatly." – Robert F. Kennedy

"If you're not prepared to be wrong, you'll never come up with anything original." – Ken Robinson

Failing well is the idea that we learn something from our mistakes. Failing well isn't a new thing. Eastern teaching points to the beginner's mindset. We have access to mountains of material on the growth and learner's mindset. It all points to the same path. Failing without learning reduces our ability to build resilience. The wrong mindset holds us back and can put us in harm's way. The opposite is the belief that there is always more to uncover about ourselves and our context.

A key learning for those like me who get into the intervention business, like coaching, mentoring, and facilitation, is that you can't help someone that doesn't want to be helped. In the early stages of building my business, I had some hard decisions to make. I set up the business on the basis that I wanted to help others. I aimed to help as many as possible. I quickly uncovered that there was a motivation gap. There was a gap between the desire to make things better and the willingness to do something about it. I developed an approach which helped build awareness of self in order to bring about the motivation to take real action. Unfortunately, I had overestimated my ability to reach people and bring them to a place where they were ready to look at building awareness of self. It took more effort and time than I was getting paid for in return. I got involved in lots of activities that didn't generate any revenue, and for a self-employed person that was a big problem. I looked at other ways of tackling the problem, like sharing ideas via blogging. That too took great amounts of time and energy that didn't materialize into revenue. So, the big decision for me was to let go of helping lots of people, for the time being. I had to bring my focus to helping a smaller group (i.e., those already doing well). These people already had the learner's mindset and were committed to life learning. I didn't give up on helping others on a grander scale, but at the time, paying the bills took a priority, which often is the reality we must face. I am not sharing this to impress or discourage you. I am simply sharing it because it is a fact of the intervention industry. The truth is that while there is an interest to really make a difference, bills must be paid. Often the help is targeted to those that can afford it or those who are willing to really go after it. This puts those that really need it at a disadvantage. Having financial means is clearly going to be a big advantage, however having a learner's mindset isn't a bad second option. This is because the learner's mindset will attract attention and that also opens doors. Through these doors I gain access to the rich and wonderful skills available to help me perform closer to my potential.

The potential for learning exists all the time, in every minute, hour, day, or week. It doesn't need to be major life events. Take this example, which showed up for me when I resumed dating after my first marriage dissolved. I had used an online network to make a date. I hadn't put a whole lot of focus into it and neither had she, as it turned out. We agreed a time and a place and met for a glass of wine. It was one of those nights with wind and rain, when you'd rather be enjoying the home comforts. The date was a disaster. She was late and we only had 45 minutes because she had made further plans later that evening. I could have been more proactive in setting up the date and made it clear that I wasn't planning on rushing off. But I didn't and I was left some ways from home at 9pm on a wet and wild Friday night with no plans. I was angry at first and tried to blame her for my predicament. A short walk in the rain cleared my head. I realized that I had not been clear in my own mind about what I wanted from the date. I'd let circumstances overtake me and I hadn't focused on what was important. At that point I stopped blaming myself or her and re-engaged with the learning opportunity. I ended up back where I should have been in the first place, warm in my own space enjoying a good movie and being grateful for who I am and what I'd achieved.

The most wonderful thing about the learner's mindset is that it is built in already. I just need to use it. A baby doesn't give up when failing to stand on two feet causes a sharp pain in the behind. The toddler doesn't stop trying to run when the sofa corner brings the show to a halt. Without focus, over time I risk losing interest in learning. They say you can't teach an old dog new tricks. You will likely see examples around you, where excessive pride or self-confidence blinds people from the facts of their situation, often leading to less than ideal experiences or even tragic consequences. You will have experienced or know of those who have fallen out of employment because their skills become redundant as the world changes. You will see complacency in day-to-day existence where the room for learning is eliminated as entertainment takes over discretionary time. The truth is that I can learn, once I remember where I started.

Failing well is a gradual process. The time to learn that fire burns is not as I step into the path of a lava flow. Feeling the heat from a birthday candle is a better place to start. Building knowledge of what is good and not so good for me in a physical sense applies equally to my internal world. Just like strengthening my arm, leg, and core muscles through exercise and workouts, I need to learn gradually. I need to strain but not tear the muscle for it to strengthen. The same goes with how I learn about math, science, writing, or any number of academic topics. Equally, I must learn gradually about myself. I must slowly peel back the layers of my understanding of who I am and what I am capable of. Major emotional trauma is fertile ground for learning; however, I risk being completely broken by it. Experiencing disappointment and hurt is a better place to start. Learning gradually about managing emotions increases my ability to cope with and recover from life's challenges. If I can't properly rationalize things that aren't where I expect them, I run the risk of falling hard, which can result in tragedy.

The retrospective

Best practice in many modern work methodologies makes use of a straightforward review to learn and grow, at the completion of a piece of work. These reviews occur no matter the outcome (i.e., successful or otherwise). These reviews typically involve the full team and take a short period of time relative to the aspect under review. For example, in the Agile Scrum methodology for developing software, a typical cycle lasts 2–3 weeks. One aspect at the end of the cycle is the retrospective review. It usually takes no more than 30–40 minutes. The key with this, and all forms of retrospectives, is that the learning potential doesn't get in the way of the momentum. Therefore, the reviews are short, focused, and done in a specific manner. The questions asked at these reviews are generally positive and focused on learning. These are some examples:

1. What worked—what can we be proud of?
2. What didn't work—what will we stop doing?
3. What could we try—what unexplored aspect might help?

The process intentionally avoids "why" questions. These types of questions invoke the need to find causes only and defocus the attention on solutions. A well-formed "What" question will inherently involve thinking about the cause but bring focus to the solution. Before answering the "What," our brains automatically join the dots on the causes to understand what did or didn't happen. With the correct "What" question our minds don't dwell on the causes.

A variation of these questions works well for personal retrospectives. For example, after failing at something, or feeling disappointed or being let down, I might ask myself:

1. What do I have—what can I be proud of or grateful for?
2. What isn't working— what should I stop doing?
3. What could I try—what steps could I take now or next time that might work better?

Life is a wonderful experience when I venture into the jungle. To survive the jungle, I need to prepare myself without over-cooking it. Half the fun is the frantic search for a tree to climb when the spear breaks.

PART 3:
PUT YOURSELF
FIRST

Chapter 12: If an oxygen mask appears in front of you, put it on before helping others!

Nurturing me

Most of us find it hard to openly commit to putting ourselves first. This is especially true for parents, or carers. I have seen the look of horror on people's faces when I say my priorities are me, my mate, my kids, and then my wider family. My conditioning told me that I should put others before myself, especially those I love, care for, and the vulnerable. Unfortunately, if I don't look after myself, I am limiting my ability to help others. When I nurture my own mental and physical wellbeing, I am better placed to nurture the wellbeing of those I care about. When I nurture and use my strengths, I radiate my potential to all those around me. It's through that process that I help others with their own wellbeing, and that is a primary source of meaning for me. So, I totally subscribe to the airline attendant safety instructions, when they tell us to put our own oxygen mask on first before helping others.

In previous chapters and in those that follow, I explore how the choices I make create my experience and bring me closer to an authentic existence. Through those choices and resulting experiences, there is one choice that haunts me. My experience is greatly impacted by who I choose to have join me on the journey. However, there is one person who is coming along, whether I like it or not. There is one person I can't choose to ignore, move away from, or sack. At 4am in the morning when all is quiet, there is only one person I can truly count on to answer the call. It's a true pickle because that person needs the support too. No matter what family, work, or social relationships I find myself operating within, there is one person that will always be there in every one of those relationships. That person is me, so I'd better get to like that person and take care of him, and I'd better do an awesome job of it! The alternative is a sad and devastating eventuality to all those wonderful people that choose to be on my journey with me.

Most parents will easily find examples where their health and wellbeing has been sacrificed for the benefit of their children. Carers will have a similar story. For years I did not exercise, had farcical engagement with my wife, had no time with my friends or extended family and made zero real downtime for myself. Before having children, I can count numerous periods where I put every moment into my work and ignored my physical wellbeing. I have countless examples where the time wasn't put into creating optimal life experiences. The distractions like alcohol and boxsets make it all too easy to do. Unfortunately, this strategy only works in the short term. Over time, the clothes got tighter, a good night's sleep seems like a distant memory, my smile was only seen in old photos, my good humor was non-existent, and it got harder and harder to find the energy needed to give my all to those I loved and cared for. This level of sacrifice put me in the back seat of Thelma and Louise's convertible roaring toward the cliff edge. While during these periods I didn't feel happy, and knew something was majorly out of alignment, I really was clueless what to do about it.

Juggling life

It amuses me to read of the growing push back against the idea of "work-life balance." It is a concept that has been bounced around for quite some time and it's something I tried to align with. However, it never sat well with me because the boundaries between "work" and "life" were always unclear for me. It is no wonder really that I found such enlightenment in David Allen's ideas, especially his definition of work, which I've adopted as "something that has meaning to me that isn't done yet." This definition makes it very hard to put nice neat boundaries around one aspect of life over another. I now prefer the idea of juggling.

There are many aspects to life. Some require lots of attention and some cause discomfort, and then there are lots of aspects that cause joy and pleasure. Life is not a balancing act—it is a juggling act. I can't juggle more than two balls. I have tried many times. For some reason my family keep buying me sets of juggling balls. Perhaps they've been saying something to me for years. No, I can't juggle balls, however, I've learned to juggle life. From what I understand of juggling balls, the key is to have strong arms and to master their movement, so that it becomes automatic, so they are in flow. Once you've mastered that, you no longer need to focus on where your arms are at. You simply focus on where the balls are, or bowling pins, or pirate swords. Mastering juggling life is the same thing. I need to be strong mentally and physically and I need to automate as much as possible. With the mechanics in flow, my mind is free to focus on where I am.

Resilience building

In my early days as a coach I focused solely on thinking and emotions, and the related behaviors. It wasn't until I started building understanding of neuroscience and resilience building, that I started to appreciate all the aspects that were needed to juggle life. Amy Brann, in her workshops and writing, has a wonderful way of building understanding of neuroscience. Brann shows that we now have evidence of how we can understand and change our behaviors and beliefs. Equally, working with Shelley Crawford and her research into resilience building allowed me to see there was a lot more to performance than just behaviors and emotions.

I would have initially thought of resilience as just the ability to "bounce back" from a major setback or loss. While it is that, it is also the ability to thrive through those challenging times. I'd often thought of resilience as something I either have or don't have. That was simply wrong. Resilience is something I build, gradually over time, through failing well as explored in chapter eleven. While I will learn from major emotional trauma, it can also send me into crazy-land. The best approach to building resilience is through learning from experiences which create strong emotions, both positive and negative.

We can identify those in our networks that seem calm and at ease in the face of major setbacks. They do have high levels of resilience, but whether through conditioning, or study, it was learned, which is wonderful news for the rest of us. To master the movement that is necessary to juggle life well, I need to tune how I think, how I feel, how I socialize, and the physical aspects of my personal experience. These four aspects are the focus of the four chapters that follow.

There is a fifth dimension. That dimension relates to how I connect everything. This dimension is explored throughout this book and summarized in the final chapter.

Rent

In the absence of rent, abundance becomes an insurmountable concept. From there, life becomes a chore.

Abundance in all that I am is a requirement of a purposeful and engaging life. It's not a "nice to have". In the absence of financial, cognitive, emotional, social, and physical abundance, I am limited in what I can do for myself and others. With an abundance of means, friendships, health, and love, my choices become vast, and unlimited. When means, friendships, health, and love come effortless to me, I am free to fully engage wholeheartedly in my purpose. When that happens, everything looks brighter, and richer. That is a life worth experiencing.

Rent is the idea that I earn something with little or no effort. To receive rent, an investment is required, and then occasional maintenance. Rent contributes to abundance and is crucial because it frees my focus and time. I will earn while being able to focus my attention on other things and engage more fully in every moment and endeavor. Furthermore, this enables me to create additional rent-getting opportunities.

The rule of rent applies to abundance in all forms. This includes the obvious like financial freedom. It also applies to having an abundance of productive employees. It applies to having an abundance of effective relationships with colleagues and those I am accountable to. It applies to having an abundance of social connections and other supportive relationships with friends and family. And finally, the rule applies to having abundance in energy, wellbeing, health, and most of all, love.

As I reflect on my journey, I realized the path was troubled and harder when there was no rent. I saw the lack of rent impacting me in many ways. I saw it in my finances, where I had to work hard for every penny. I saw it as an employee where I felt incompetent and out of my depth, and where relationships felt confrontational and conflictual. I saw it as a manager where direct reports struggled with their tasks and what we needed to get done together. I saw the lack of rent impacting my business development as my network failed to deliver enough new sales. I saw it when I played team sports and I felt lethargic and like a burden. I saw it in my friendships, where I felt alone, and unappreciated. I saw it as a parent where I felt out of my depth and started to resent the rewards of my choices.

It's clear to me now that my failing was in the lack of investment. Without that investment of appropriate amount of time and resources, rent is unrealistic. Without rent, every thing and every moment must be earned, repeatedly, every time. And that becomes tiring and a burden.

When I under-invested in my knowledge and skills, I had limited choices of jobs and I struggled to find fulfillment in the roles I secured. When I poorly invested excess earnings, I made little headway. When I under-invested in nurturing my employees I had limited time to grow the business, as I worked constantly to monitor and adjust their path. When I under-invested in giving my time unconditionally to those in my network, they became distant and non-responsive. When I under-invested in exercise and healthy eating, I couldn't enjoy team sports or physical activities. When I under-invested in appreciating and making quality time for friends, family, and my partner, I got little love back. When I under-invested in my parenting and took the easy option, my children misbehaved.

When I invested in my knowledge and skills, I had opportunities put before me without asking. When I invested earnings more appropriately, I had richer options later. When I nurtured those that worked with me, their work aligned better with who they were and what we needed to achieve together. When I invested in helping and making time for those in my network, new business opportunities became more numerous and more fruitful. When I invested in regular exercise and more appropriate eating, I felt energetic, and better able to think clearer and more positively. When I made quality time for loved ones, I saw joy and meaning in so many more interactions. When I focused on being a good parent, not their best friend, my children rewarded me with laughter and love.

Every investment resulted in receiving more than I needed with little or no effort on my part. Every investment resulted in rent.

Chapter 13: Thinking it through

My biggest critic and my biggest fan

The voices in my head are both my biggest critics and my biggest fans. My favorite representation of the little friend in my head is done by Johnny Depp in character as Jack Sparrow in the *Pirates of the Caribbean* movies. It's when he talks to his good and bad side. Two miniature Jacks, in all their pirate glory, appear on either shoulder then whisper into his ear. One mini Jack is encouraging him to think of himself. The other is encouraging him to look at the wider consequences. It's a wonderful depiction of the constant conversation that goes on within our own heads. Talking things over in our head is a critical part of our existence. It is essential to engaging effectively with our world. There is a flaw in Jack Sparrow's council. The flaw is that it is too simplistic. We typically have many variations of our "mini-me" floating around our heads, all talking, often at the same time.

The voices in my head appraise everything I see, hear, smell, touch, and taste. The voices also appraise my feelings and my memories. That appraisal process influences how I act or react to how I experience the world. Even when I am talking to someone else, getting their advice, I am still interpreting, and reframing what they share into my own version of the truth. I form all number of associations with everything that comes to me. It's this stuff that forms the basis of my self-talk. It's this stuff that causes me to believe that I am both my biggest critic and my biggest fan, all at the same time.

We've all been asked "what are you thinking?" I certainly have, but now I make a conscious effort not to ask that question, firstly, and foremost, because it's none of my business. Secondly, the answer is never what they were thinking. The answer is usually "nothing" or something to that effect, which is simply not true and we both know it. That causes unnecessary tension, when the question should have been something like "I am nervous, not sure of myself, and would like to engage with you to understand why." The fact is that we are always thinking, whether we are conscious of it or not. Even as you read this paragraph, you are processing and thinking, trying to understand it and relate it to your own experience. Besides, the answer can't be what they were thinking when I asked them what they were thinking. This is because the question interrupts the thinking process. After the interruption, all the person can generally think about is why I asked the question. At this point, the internal defenses go up and the response is of no value to me or the person I am asking. I'll get to that further in this chapter. For now, let's accept that we are always thinking. The key to moving to a more authentic existence is to be in control of our thinking, when we need to.

Set the stage

While we are always thinking, our mind has a serious limitation that can severely hamper our ability to perform. The limitation is simply in the way we think. As with all limitations, understanding them allows us to manage or negate the impact on our ability to perform at our best.

To help explain this limitation I like David Rock's metaphor of the prefrontal cortex. In his book *Your Brain at Work: Strategies for Overcoming Distraction, Regaining Focus, and Working Smarter All Day Long*, Rock presents the idea of a theater. The stage of the theater is the prefrontal cortex, the part of the brain that we use for thought. In order to think we bring actors onto the stage and have them interact. The actors can come from outside the theater (i.e., the outer world) or the audience (i.e., our inner world). The inner world is our memories. To use our memories in our thinking we need to find them and bring them up onto the stage. The order of the seating of the audience represents how recently we have had that memory on the stage, i.e., in our conscious thoughts. Older memories will find themselves way up the back in the dark and may take some time to be found. This helps explain why that movie name that escaped us during dinner over the weekend suddenly pops into our mind during a meeting on Tuesday afternoon. To make sense of our thoughts we need the actors on the stage long enough for us to compare them and make value judgments. And here is the clincher—while the seated area of the theater is infinitely large, the stage is not. In fact, the stage can only hold focus on one thing at a time. When I share this idea, I usually get someone mentioning multi-tasking, and how one sex is better than the other at it. Unfortunately, while this may be true, our prefrontal cortex is the same. We can only focus our conscious thought on one thing at any one time. I like to think of multi-tasking as the activity of swapping things on and off the stage. Someone who can quickly swap actors on and off the stage may be a good multi-tasker. However, not giving the actors enough time on stage also translates to poor decision making.

When I take an active role in how I use my "stage" I have a better chance of ensuring it is used for the things that bring me closer to where I want to be, not further away. Another way of thinking of this is a theater production without a director. When there is no director, the production depends entirely on the quality of the script and the ability of the actors and support crew to "play along nicely". This idea also assumes a nice and controlled environment, where the audience behaves, and the stage doors are well managed. By the doors I mean the million and one ways we can receive new information and emotions in our complex realities. Even if I was to lock myself away in a dark, sound-proofed, padded room with no devices, I simply can't escape my thoughts. The director then, in terms of our own minds, is the part of our conscious mind which is aware of our thoughts and where our attention is.

We are under attack!

I love to think of myself as a rational, balanced individual, who holds himself up to a high standard in how I present myself and interact with the world. It's a love and a dream, because it's not possible for me or anyone, at least, not all the time. There are many times when I've been out of control. It's a feeling like someone else is driving the bus, or, in the theater analogy, the feeling that a guest director has stepped in with a completely new script and is reorganizing things to their liking, not mine. Thankfully, I now understand why this happens.

Our brains can be thought of in terms of three main parts, the lower or reptilian part, the middle, or mammalian part and the upper or human part. Each is aptly named because of the characteristic of each that we share with said creatures.

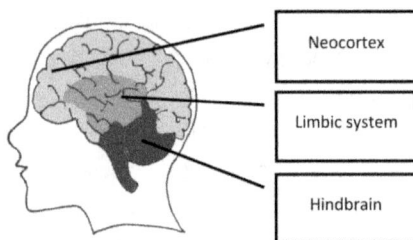

Neocortex

Limbic system

Hindbrain

The reptilian part, or as it's known more technically, the hindbrain, includes the brain stem, and our autonomic nervous system. This part of the brain is associated with "freeze, fight or flight." My kids and I prefer to describe this part of the brain as the "Do I eat it, or does it eat me?" part. This lower part is concerned with survival. It is known as the reptilian part because its functions are shared with reptiles and all other creatures that have evolved along the same path.

The middle or mammalian part, or also known as the limbic system, is the emotional center. It is here within this middle part that we have emotions and feelings, an essential aspect to bonding with each other and, as it is with all mammals, bonding with our young.

The upper part, the human part, also known as the neocortex, is the thinking, or rational part of our brain. It is within this part of the brain that we process and evaluate the inputs we receive and decide what to do about them. This is our theater stage.

Connected to the three parts of the brain is the amygdala. While small, the amygdala plays a very important part in that its primary purpose is to help us survive. It is a kind of radar, which has the job of looking out for possible

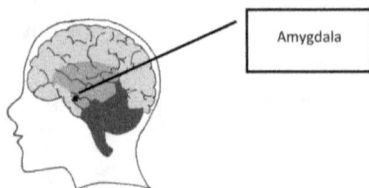

Amygdala

threats. How it works is that it takes the inputs generated from our senses and events around us and searches our memories for close matching patterns.

Once it finds a close enough match it can take over the functions of the brain and force that memory onto our actions.

Having a fast and efficient way to react is good if our senses have picked up a fast-approaching ball on the pitch that needs to be caught or a dog dashing out in front of the car that needs to be avoided.

This capability is not so good if our sensors have picked up an action, comment, and tone that has caused us pain in the past. It is not so good because it is rare that past situations of this nature are the same as the present. And in most personal and professional situations, actions and comments from others require thought before a response is warranted. However, if the amygdala can do its job, it will block out the upper brain and take over and the response and action will be driven from things we have experienced in the past. The amygdala has no ability to reassess the present or adapt. It is purely a reactive function and executes what worked previously.

This is the Amygdala Hijack: a situation where we act based on what happened in the past and completely stop considering anything new or different and anything specific to the present moment. Amygdala Hijack is a term coined by Daniel Goleman in his 1996 book, *Emotional Intelligence: Why It Can Matter More Than IQ*.

Once in a Hijack, we will be irrational. We will not be able to communicate effectively. We may withdraw, we may get aggressive and will likely do and say things that we wouldn't do if we had the opportunity to think about it.

Another worrying thing about the Hijack is that it can last for long periods. The Hijack typically lasts for a few moments, but it also can last for hours, days, weeks. This happens when the emotion to memory association is so strong that we accept it as being normal. This blocks our rational thinking for long periods of time. It's not that we are irrational from that moment on, it's just that we make a habit of applying the memory instantly. We get so used to the pattern and response, that we make a habit of it. We can operate quite rationally for most of the time, but the instant the situation arises again we go straight into that irrational place.

We all have experienced an Amygdala Hijack. We have experienced them ourselves and we will be subject to others experiencing them. A child's tantrum, someone losing their temper, or someone going silent in a meeting are all examples. There are plenty more. The Amygdala Hijack turns perfectly normal people into crazy people. It impacts both personal and professional aspects of our lives. However, there is hope! The Amygdala Hijack can be prevented. We can learn to manage our thinking and avoid them entirely.

The good news is that, the upper, or thinking part of our brain can shut down the amygdala before it can take over. Inputs from our senses and events around us are simultaneously provided to both the amygdala and the upper brain. In the upper brain we can then consider the situation and choose what to do about it. So, the key is to catch the associated emotion and start thinking consciously about it before the amygdala gets up to speed. This conscious thought will quieten the amygdala and leave our rational side in control. Quietening the amygdala isn't hard, however there are two conditions that must be met. I'll get to both of those later in the chapter.

Flowing into the right script

I love the idea of Flow as largely associated with the work of Mihaly Csikszentmihalyi. I am including a short mention of Csikszentmihalyi for two reasons. Firstly, being able to pronounce Csikszentmihalyi is an example of the point of this section—you feel in Flow when you can master pronouncing it. Secondly, Csikszentmihalyi is one of the founding fathers of modern psychology (i.e., positive psychology). The study of positive psychology went against the norms of psychology in the day, because it didn't just bring focus to the study of us many broken people. It brought focus to the study of the successful. In Csikszentmihalyi's cornerstone research in the early stages of positive psychology, he studied the behaviors of hundreds of successfully creative people. He studied people that had had significant cultural impact. He studied scientists, artists, writers, educators, politicians, social activists, engineers, and religious leaders. What he found became largely known as Flow.

Flow is mastery of a skill or domain. It's a place where I lose sense of time and space as I do something truly rewarding and productive in terms of impact or output. Flow is where I am so absorbed in creating and maintaining the conditions for that spectacularly beautiful experience that I engage with it fully and without resistance. It's the seamless performance of dozens of dancers or the "crack" of a perfectly hit golf ball or the sharing of belly-aching laughter with our children. Flow is where there is perfect alignment between potential and utilization of a capability. It is where I fully understand the skills I have, and I fully engage them.

From a practical viewpoint, Flow requires learning and practice, from both a physical and cognitive sense. I need to build the physical skills in my strength and automotive functions. I also need to get my head together, and that is much easier said than done.

I am not a golfer. I have played golf. I even still have a set of clubs. The last time they were used was a couple of years ago when I lent them to a friend. It was during the time that I tried to take up golf that I experienced flow, or lack of it. It frustrated me that I was able to hit the ball well on occasions but mostly it went flying off in random directions. That resulted in far too much time spent scouring bushes at the side of the course. It annoyed me that I was able to hit it well sometimes but not all the time. Surely, if I could hit the ball well once, I could do it all the time? I found the answer to that question, in the works by Timothy Gallwey. Gallwey's book, "*The Inner Game of Tennis*" written in 1974, builds on the notion of "Potential" and "Performance." He explains that there is a gap. The gap is the thoughts which we have when going about an activity. In other words, the gap is interference. Gallwey's resulting formula is "performance is equal to potential less interference."

I exist in a world of interference. Interference from others was typically the place I focused my concerns, however it's not the biggest risk to my ability to achieve Flow. It's the self-doubt, fear, and other negative emotions that hold me back. For a golfer, the test for this is simple. They just leave their phone in the club room, go onto the course alone, put earplugs in their ears and play. No matter how hard they try to remove all external distractions and interference, they'll still have their own thoughts along for the ride, getting in the way of Flow.

The answer, as uncovered by Csikszentmihalyi, and other key players in positive psychology, like Martin Seligman, is to know myself better. Specifically, I need to know my skills. I need to know what I value and my strengths. It's from that place of knowledge that I build confidence and from there I keep the negative emotions at bay. This knowledge helps me maintain control of my amygdala and bring me to a Flow stage more often.

Valued strengths

The idea of authenticity has fascinated me for some time. I am fascinated as to how choices about where I put myself, and what I do when I get there, impacts how I experience the world, if at all. The process of exploring choices brought me to values and strengths (also known as traits). Even after applying some knowledge of who I was and what I did well, I still found myself repeating the same limiting pattern. For ten years I repeated a pattern of chasing after that "next great job" only to be disillusioned with it after 12 to 18 months. The insight only really came once I started to explore what was behind my decisions (i.e., my values and strengths).

At our core, the core of our personality, are values, and strengths. While they may shift around a little as we progress through life, fundamentally they are who we are from our teenage years, and they now drive every aspect of how we behave and respond. Values and strengths are at the core of how we experience the world around us. As explored in chapter six, we use beliefs to drive behaviors, consciously, and unconsciously. We use beliefs to evaluate our experiences, and this directly influences our sense of progress and achievement. Also, in a sense, beliefs encompass our goals in that goals represent the desired future state of something that we believe to be important. Therefore, values and strengths are at the core of how we act and how we evaluate the experiences we have.

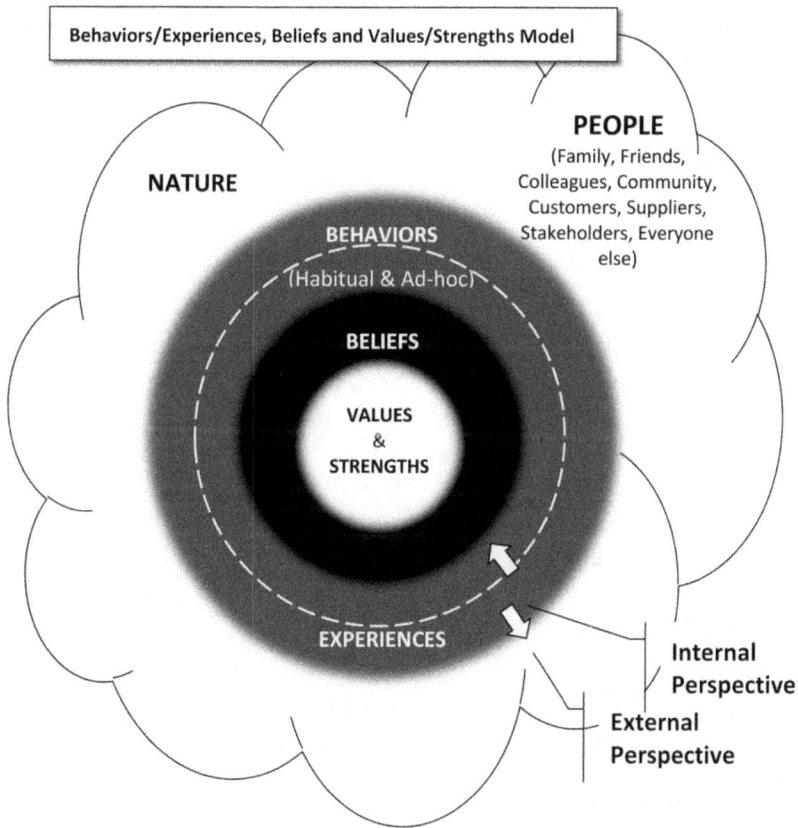

Behaviors/Experiences, Beliefs and Values/Strengths Model

NATURE

PEOPLE
(Family, Friends, Colleagues, Community, Customers, Suppliers, Stakeholders, Everyone else)

BEHAVIORS
(Habitual & Ad-hoc)

BELIEFS

VALUES & STRENGTHS

EXPERIENCES

Internal Perspective

External Perspective

Values are the elements of our identity that give meaning, mission, and purpose to our lives. We base our decisions on them and therefore they energize and motivate us to do things. Values are concepts like wisdom, freedom, openness, connection, personal growth, affiliation, etc. Once I clarified my true values, I found that it was easier to make decisions. I found that understanding values was like learning to read the compass that has been helping me navigate through life. The thing that I found most interesting was that we don't operate via a simple list of values. Instead we use a complex matrix, driven by context, and the level of importance. The level of importance of one value over another, impacts how strongly we are motivated toward or away from a decision or experience.

As I started to better understand my values, I found I was behaving and responding differently to situations at work and in my personal life. By better understanding what I value within these situations I have been better able to manage my emotions and therefore respond more appropriately. More appropriate responses made it easier to build and maintain my relationships and get me places I hadn't been able to go before.

Strengths, or personality traits, are generally defined as enduring patterns of perceiving, relating to, and thinking. That all relates to both our environment and how we see ourselves. In other words, they are the building blocks of our belief system. Strengths would include being passive versus assertive, cautious versus lively, spontaneous versus dutiful, reserved versus personable, etc.

Knowing my strengths was a crucial step in creating a new pattern of behavior with respect to my career. Leveraging what I am good at has me being more productive and therefore of greater value to the work I do. It also has me doing things that align with the stronger parts of my personality, and that feels good. This helps me feel better about myself. Feeling better about myself contributes directly to a more positive state of mind. Operating within a more positive state not only helps me build better and stronger relationships, but it also helps me see opportunities that I was blinded to previously.

The exploration of mastery of a domain of knowledge or skill, brought me to Authentic Happiness, an initiative founded by Martin Seligman. Authentic Happiness is based on the idea that we excel or operate in the flow state, when we are using our stronger strengths. These are also referred to as our Signature Strengths. The idea here is that as individuals we have varied learned or natural abilities across twenty-four strengths. Examples of these include Creativity, Bravery, Kindness, Leadership, and Humor. The research shows us that when we engage the five or so stronger strengths, we are more likely to be in Flow. Equally, when we are required to leverage some of the weaker strengths, we struggle with our energy and focus. The key, therefore, is to know our stronger strengths and use them as much as possible. Also, knowing where we aren't as strong is crucial, as it allows us to manage it. For example, if Humor was a stronger strength and Bravery wasn't, and yet we were required to enter a situation that required Bravery, we could use Humor before and after the situation to lift our energy and reduce the impact of having to work much harder.

Moving to a better me

If we accept our behaviors and how we evaluate our experiences is largely driven by our beliefs, and we accept that this in turn is based on our values and strengths, then moving to a more authentic representation of ourselves is simply a matter of uncovering our values and strengths. With that awareness we can breakdown or reinforce our beliefs. Once in full awareness of our beliefs we can directly influence the behaviors and valuation we want to engage. Coaching, be it self-coaching, or with help, allows us to build that awareness.

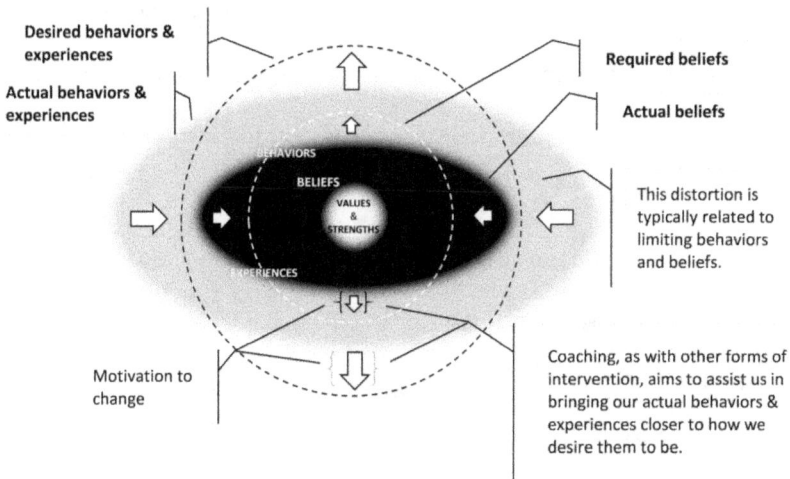

Building awareness of strengths is simply a matter of observing our behavior. Like peeling layers of an onion, while straightforward, it does take effort, and time. Removing one layer of the onion allows us to get at the next layer. With each new understanding comes a new perspective.

In self-studying my behaviors, I engage two parallel activities. The first activity is to spend time considering what I do well and where that is serving me. The steps for this are below. The other parallel activity is to observe my daily routines and practices and reflect on the skills I am deploying.

These questions help surface strengths:

What am I good at?

What are my dominant gifts?

What am I best at?

What natural abilities do I possess?

What do I do that gets a positive response from people I respect?

What do I do that does not seem like work, regardless of the difficulty?

What do I do that causes doors to open with ease for me?

What excites me?

What activities do I enjoy the most at work, at home, or in social situations?

What am I passionate about?

What do I love spending time on?

What desires keep tugging at my heart?

What motivates me when I am most productive?

What do I do that makes me feel good emotionally and spiritually?

You can also obtain your stronger strengths by taking the 45-minute *Signature Strength Survey*, as part of University of Pennsylvania's *Authentic Happiness* work. It can be found at https://www.authentichappiness.sas.upenn.edu/. You will need to register to take the test. Your details will be held confidentially, however your answers will, anonymously, be used to extend and grow the research body. After registering, go to *Questionnaires*, select *VIA Survey of Character Strengths*. Take the test and then extract the results. When you get your results, make sure you extract all 25 (i.e., choose "Show More" after Strength #5). You will also find great value in the Gallup StrengthFinder 2.0. You might even have an intervention professional, like a coach, help you understand your strengths using psychometric tools that study traits (i.e., Psytech International's 15FQ+). Having someone else help you understand what you are good at is very efficient, but self-study and self-assessment can be just as effective.

Unlike building awareness of strengths, building awareness of values is not straightforward. It is harder because our values are largely a function of our subconscious mind. This is because often we operate with beliefs that we have built around the values. These beliefs are often well established and sometimes not even our own, as discussed in chapter six. My journey to understanding my values started when I studied coaching and mentoring, progressed greatly through being coached, and is an ongoing and sometimes frightening experience. It is for this reason that I believe the most effective way to understand values is by working with a coach or therapist. However, as outlined below, there are some things that can be achieved with self-study.

To uncover my own values, without help, I explored and tested my past experiences, and then looked at what I valued during those times. The steps are as follows:

(1) First, on a large piece of blank paper I write a list of experiences. I consider where I have made a difficult decision or took an unpopular course of action. I look for times when in my heart, I knew it needed to happen. I look for times when I went against the advice of those I held dear. I also look at experiences where I have made a decision, gone with it but still didn't feel right about it. I list the experiences down the page.

(2) Next, I expand the list by considering what else drives my decisions. I consider what behaviors I find it difficult to tolerate, cause discomfort, or create stress for me. I look for the opposite of that behavior and add it to my list. For example, I might get annoyed at drivers who don't let me merge into traffic. For this I would write the opposite as "Drivers allowing me to merge into traffic."

(3) For each item I listed on the page, I write next to it the values that were behind the decision or that experience. Below is a list of values to help with that process. These are just a guide, and at times, I come up with my own word or phrase to represent the value behind that decision or experience.

Ability	Acceptance	Accomplishment	Achievement
Acknowledgement	Action	Activity	Adaptability
Adventure	Aliveness	Aloneness	Altruism
Appearance	Approval	Art	Autonomy
Balance	Beauty	Calmness	Caring for others
Challenge	Change	Charity	Clarity
Comfort	Commitment	Communication	Community
Compassion	Competition	Complexity	Confidentiality
Connection	Consistency	Contribution	Courage
Creativity	Curiosity	Decisiveness	Difference
Dignity	Ecology	Elegance	Empathy
Entertainment	Excellence	Excitement	Exploration
Fairness	Faith	Family	Fascination
Flexibility	Forgiveness	Fortitude	Freedom

Friendship	Fulfilment	Fun	Generosity
Giving	Glory	Goals	Gratefulness
Growth	Happiness	Harmony	Health
Helpfulness	Helping	Humor	Honesty
Hope	Impact	Independence	Influence
Innovation	Integrity	Intelligence	Intimacy
Joy	Justice	Kindness	Knowledge
Laughter	Leadership	Learning	Leisure
Life	Love	Loyalty	Mastery
Meaning	Money	Music	Nature
Novelty	Openness	Order	Organization
Passion	Patience	Peacefulness	Perseverance
Personal growth	Playfulness	Pleasing others	Pleasing self
Pleasure	Positivity	Power	Privacy
Purpose	Recognition	Relationship(s)	Relaxation
Resilience	Respect	Respite	Responsibility
Rest	Safety	Security	Self-confidence
Self-discipline	Self-love	Self-reliance	Serenity
Service	Sex	Simplicity	Spirituality
Spontaneity	Sport	Stamina	Status
Staying power	Stimulating change	Stimulation	Strength
Structure	Success	Support	Survival

Teamwork	Tidiness	Tolerance	Trust
Understanding	Uniqueness	Using my abilities	Variety
Vitality	Wealth	Wisdom	Zest

(4) Next, I extract the list of values onto a separate piece of paper, removing any duplicates. I write one value per line, down the left side of the page.

(5) Now I reflect on the values I have extracted. I give myself time to consider what I have written. When done, I get a ruler, and draw two lines down the page, to make three columns. The first column should contain my list of values. I label the second column "Priorities" and the third column "Honoring."

(6) Using the list of values, I consider where these exist in my current situation, in terms of priority. In the middle column, I will give each value a number, where one represents my highest priority. I try numbering my top five first, then move into the next five, and so on. Each value must be given a unique number (i.e., I cannot have two "priority one" values) I number them from one to the total number of values I have listed. When I am done, I take time to reflect on what I see in front of me.

(7) Finally, I take my list of values and assess how well I am honoring that value in my life right now. Using the rightmost column, for each value, I give them a number between one and ten. Giving a "ten" means that I am honoring that value in EVERY decision I make and in EVERY situation at present. Giving a "one" means I am not honoring this value at all right now. With the "Honoring" list I can have duplicates, i.e., I can award "ten" to any number of my values.

To verify my self-assessment, I keep it close to me over a period, perhaps over the course of the next seven days. When I make decisions, I check the list. I see if the value behind my decision is represented. I check to see if my priority and honoring numbering still holds true.

When guiding clients through this process, I then ask them to look at where they are not honoring high priority values. For example, scoring a five or lower in "Honoring" against a value in the top five priorities, may represent a value that I am allowing to be squashed or put aside. It could be an indicator of a set of circumstances that I am not happy with and need to change. I would ask my clients to consider the price they are paying for that value not being honored, by which I mean the cost to their physical and emotional wellbeing. To move forward, I suggest my clients consider what it would take to increase the "honoring" number for this value.

Keeping crazy at bay

Quietening and keeping the amygdala in check is essential to staying in control and avoiding resembling a crazy person. As mentioned earlier in this chapter, to put the amygdala back to sleep, my upper brain needs to start thinking consciously about my emotions before the amygdala has found a close enough match. Once the match is found it is very hard to persuade the amygdala away from its designed purpose.

To start consciously thinking about my emotions, two conditions need to be met. The first condition is that I need to be aware of my emotions and know what to do with them. This is the concept of emotional intelligence and will be explored further in the next chapter. The other condition relates to busyness. If the emotion is particularly strong the amygdala will find a close match very quickly (i.e., in fractions of seconds). The problem here is that if my upper brain is busy, it won't be able to capture the emotion in time and start thinking about it before the amygdala does its job.

Having the ability to observe my emotions and then know what to do about them is, however, of no value if the mind is too busy thinking about other things. As David Allen suggests, we aren't talking about information overload or overwhelm, we are simply talking about an exponential increase in the rate of change. This rate of change is not matched by the skills acquired growing up (i.e., there is a gap in the skills needed to manage the complexities in life). Below are examples of where skills and complexity collide:

200 new emails appearing each day

A calendar of back to back meetings

An exponentially growing list of really important things

Faces of those let down by someone turning up late

Needing to find new excuses for the missed commitments

For a large part of my early career I subscribed to the idea that a busy mind was a good thing. Thinking translated to active engagement and that was how stuff got done. I didn't appreciate that to perform at my best, the kind of thinking was also important, not just the act itself. The experience that clearly showed me the dangers happened at the kitchen sink doing the dishes. I had a major project underway at work, and it was preoccupying my mind. I was doing the dishes as I worked out solutions to the various challenges that the project was facing. I was happy and content, away in my thoughts as I cleaned the pots and pans. Then things started to get harder. My thinking was getting interrupted. I had this nagging feeling. Then it contained a physical element. There was a noise and a pulling at the side of my trouser leg. I turned and shouted "WHAT." I had to look down at this point as the source of the distraction was only knee high. It was my four-year old son, now with a startled, scared expression, and on the brink of bursting into tears. Thankfully for me, in the face of my angry outburst he still found the courage to repeat himself. He simply said, "Look Daddy, I drew this for you." It broke my heart and gave me the catalyst to find answers. From there I started to explore how to get everything out of my head and use my thinking capacity more effectively.

To perform at my best, I need to do everything I can to keep my thinking mind clear and ready. In this state, I have the capacity to effectively process, and then respond appropriately, to everything coming at me.

The lack of skills in managing the complexity impacts performance, and that impacts productivity. The evidence of this is in the existence of the Amygdala

Hijack. All we need to do is measure, in ourselves and those around us, the frequency at which the Amygdala Hijack occurs. Unless we are talking about life-threatening situations, an Amygdala Hijack is a good indicator that the mind has been too busy to efficiently process an emotion. Every time an Amygdala Hijack occurs there is a strong possibility that someone isn't being rational or isn't performing with full awareness of the specific situation. The resulting decisions are often inappropriate and create more work in undoing or repairing the fallout. That extra work impacts productivity. It is where days appear to roll into one another with seemingly little forward momentum.

In chapter twenty, I explore how I leverage the awareness of what I do well and what I value, to reduce the craziness I experience.

114

Chapter 14: Because I care

Unlocking the potential of emotions

Emotions are indicators of something in our experience of the world that we should move closer to or further away from. The strength of the emotion gives the level of importance in our mind and the speed at which we should move.

When we think of emotions, there will be a few big-ticket names that always get a mention, like love, hate, and fear. However, while research has ways of categorizing and grouping them, they all play in our minds and both enable and hinder our journey. To make things a little easier, I like to focus on the two sides of the same coin (i.e., negative and positive emotions).

Examples of negative emotions include fear, disgust, boredom, hate, envy, sorrow, anger, frustration, annoyance, discontentment, alarm, anxiety, guilt, and indifference.

Examples of positive emotions include joy, love, happiness, gratitude, serenity, interest, hope, pride, amusement, inspiration, awe, elevation (from acts of kindness), altruism (from selfless giving), satisfaction, relief, affection, cheerfulness, surprise (good), confidence (self-efficacy), admiration, enthusiasm, eagerness, euphoria, peacefulness, and optimism.

Emotions are the basis of our freeze, flight, or fight response managed by the amygdala, as explored in chapter thirteen. Equally, emotions are a key input to our managed thinking in the human part of our brain. Emotions both keep us safe and put us in danger. Emotions hold us back from engaging fully and helping others. Emotions drive selfless giving and sacrifice. Emotions enable us to engage passionately with a specific subject or experience. Emotions are the fuel that brings us toward and through our challenges. Emotions are the glue that brings us into and out of connection and bonds with our fellow human beings.

Skill in being aware of emotions and knowing what to do with them (i.e., emotional intelligence), is crucial to success in having a better experience of the world. At the heart of this skill in observing emotions in ourselves and others, is the ability to observe our thinking as we experience the world, as explored in chapter thirteen. Being conscious of my thoughts and actions is important because it allows me to engage my thinking brain, and once I do that I am in control. Once the prefrontal cortex is engaged, I need to know what to do with those emotions. Key to that is my understanding of what I value and my strengths. It is important to have this understanding, so that when something comes before me, I have a better than average chance of knowing what to do with it.

Catching emotions

Emotional intelligence can be taught, and improved with practice. A great place to start is naming emotions. This is the technique of using my self-talk to my advantage, and there isn't much to it. I simply use a phrase like "I am feeling excited" or "I am feeling fearful" or "I am feeling angry." Saying it quietly in my head is enough. Saying it out loud can help also, particularly if that emotion is strong. The technique is enhanced by repeating it over and over, until I feel a sense of calm and control returning. Once that sense of calm and control returns, my thinking brain is back in the driver's seat. Once I am in that place, I can look at the emotion and its meaning for me. Clearly, none of this works if I can't observe the emotion in the first place. Practice is the key to that. It's best to start small and built up.

My most extreme example of using this naming technique came during a three-way meeting. It occurred when someone I cared about shared a whole raft of untruths about my behavior. The deluge of lies was emotional and intense. I felt like shouting and defending each one immediately. However, overreacting would have simply given fuel to the lies. Telling myself repeatedly that "I was scared and angry" was key to holding my tongue and collecting my thoughts. I must have repeated that thirty times. Eventually calm returned, and I was able to respond to these allegations with clarity and logic. Rather than making things worse for myself, I was able to show the lies for what they were. I was able to help move things in a more positive and constructive direction.

To build the skill, I started with naming emotions in normal situations, like joy, and contentment. I named these in my mind when I felt them and then explored how the mind reacted to thinking about them. There is an art to observing our thinking, but it's an art that we are already able to do, and we can perfect it with practice. This practice is explored further as part of building the attention muscle at the end of chapter eighteen.

Caring

The easiest way I've found to manage strong emotions is to tell myself that they are with me because I care. When I am feeling nervous, I know it is because something is important to me. When I am feeling scared, I know it is because I don't want to let myself or others down. When I am feeling angry, I know it's because my expectations haven't been met. When I feel love, I know I am engaged in something of meaning. When I am feeling excited, I know it is something engaging and important to me.

When I coach, I ask my clients "how does that make you feel?" Through the conversation, I encourage them to look for what they care about with respect to those emotions. The resulting conversation is rich and engaging.

When I see strong emotions at play with my kids, I get down to their eye level and ask them to express how they feel. When they are fighting with each other, I get down to their level and ask them how the other might feel. They don't usually respond with much, but their behavior does change. Suggesting they "think" triggers the prefrontal cortex. A lovely example of this was when I intervened in an argument my daughters were having. They both wanted to be the one to clean the whiteboard in the playroom. I simply asked each to describe what the other was feeling at that moment. They looked at me blankly. Nothing was said for about 40 seconds. We all just stared at each other. Then they turned away from me and started discussing together how they could both clean the whiteboard and what was needed. It was like magic.

When my kids express negative emotions and struggle to see past their fear, anger, nerves, or frustration, I tell them that it is perfectly okay and good to feel this way. I tell them it is okay, because they care. The calming effect is immediate.

The same goes for my relationships with adults, though I don't usually need to get down to their eye level.

Reframing my experience of emotions as "because I care," opens a whole new level of self-talk. I can then think about what I am experiencing and what it means to me. It's through this self-talk that emotions get managed.

Fighting the right cause

Negative emotions, like anger and frustration, are both a powerful friend and foe in the fight against the behaviors that hold me back. Giving into and avoiding truths about my own mental state is both a cause of harm and loss of learning opportunity. Unfortunately, the cards are stacked against us. Some communities struggle to deal with negative emotions properly because few want to acknowledge their own disappointments. People often prefer to say nothing and keep working and looking for distractions to hide the pain. By distraction I am referring to engaging in substance abuse, obsessive sports, volunteering etc. This is done instead of truly facing the negative emotions. When I allow myself to experience the emotions properly, I can use them to drive my energy and focus toward the changes I need to make to myself and the context I operate within. I can also use these emotions to fight.

Fighting is an important aspect of our survival. Among other things, it helps us stand up for ourselves, a skill that has helped us over the ages achieve many things. As well as defending what we have, over the ages fighting has helped our ancestors get fed and win that prized partner so we can procreate. Fighting doesn't come without its problems, specifically in the modern world when the response being invoked as a result of the Amygdala Hijack. Just being in control of my negative emotions isn't enough to function productively. As with all emotions, I need to channel the associated energy somewhere appropriate. I found two methods that have really helped me channel my negative emotions. Firstly, I got a punching bag. Even two minutes of pounding the bag brings a whole new focus to my energy. The second approach I do while exercising. I bring my negative emotions to my attention and use the Rocky Balboa style air-punching, and sometimes cursing, to vent my unneeded negative energy. Clearly, I need to be mindful of where I do this. When I control my negative emotions, I bring the focus back to something I can use. I can use it to fight the right cause.

To understand negative emotions, as with all my emotions, I simply need to bring them to my conscious mind and then explore what it means to me. This process is greatly aided by talking with a supportive friend, being coached, and using counseling/psychotherapy. Acknowledgment of the negative emotion is the first step. Once in that awareness, I must own it and experience it. From there I can shake it off and drive forward. I can help myself by looking for the opposite and what it would take to reach that place. From the dark I come back into the light.

Negative emotions, when explored properly, serve three purposes. Firstly, they are an excellent motivator in that they give me something to fight for. Secondly, in exploring the negative emotions, I uncover the limiting, or borrowed beliefs as explored in Part one. That awareness enables me to be my true authentic self. And finally, mastery in managing my own emotions is going to make it much easier to help others manage theirs, especially those I care about.

Deliberately positive

Knowing only positive experiences, engaging only with loving, and caring people and having everything always where it needs to be, is the stuff of fairy tales. Life just isn't like that. Life is full of negativity and negative experiences. Negativity around me also creates near perfect conditions for the Amygdala Hijack. However, how I engage with the crappy side of life is a choice.

Removing myself from negative circumstances and distancing myself from people who invoke strong emotions, is lovely in theory. Sure, I could change jobs, leave the soccer club, move to a different city or stop spending time with a negative friend. However, I won't and can't remove the potential entirely. I will always have to endure potentially derailing behavior from friends, family members, colleagues, those in my communities, or important business contacts.

Angry, miserable people want us to be drawn into their misery so that they feel less alone with it. Left unmanaged it is potentially catastrophic. In the body of work pioneered by Vilayanur Ramachandran, we mirror the emotions of others. I find that when I don't protect my own positive state, I can easily get caught up in everything about their problems and start compromising on who I am and what I want to be.

I use one of three strategies for dealing with long-term negativity from those I care about or must deal with for professional reasons. Those are confronting, ignoring, and deliberate positivity.

Confronting: In dealing with negativity, I have tried confronting the behavior, but that only got me so far. I've found that confronting negativity is only worthwhile if the other party is in a place of seeing growth as a possibility. If they aren't ready to learn and forgive themselves, the confronting approach won't help. In certain situations, confronting can even cause more harm and make things more challenging. For example, standing up to a skilled bully can have me looking like the aggressor and have the bully looking like the victim. This doesn't serve anyone.

Ignoring: At times I have also given into the temptation to turn away and ignore those continually expressing negativity. That helps in the short term. However, I found that by ignoring them, I am buying into their misery. That causes more hurt for me than dealing with the hurt caused by the misery they inflict.

Deliberate Positivity: In his book *Talking to Crazy: How to Deal with the Irrational and Impossible People in Your Life*, Mark Goulston explores various forms of irrational behavior. As well as helping to understand the irrational behavior, he provides details on how to manage ourselves in these situations. Goulston also shares ideas on how we can help the other person get to a better place. Exploring Goulston's insights gave me the confidence to explore this third option. To counteract negative behavior, I try to be over-the-top with positivity and I do it constantly and deliberately. As often as I can, I start by asking the person how they are. Or in a professional context, I ask "How are things going for you?" I do it in a positive and cheerful manner. Then when they reply with the usual, "I'm tired," "I'm not well," "I've got loads to do," or whatever it is, I empathize. For example, I say, "That must be terrible for you," or something like that. I then change the subject to something positive, and perhaps unrelated to the concern expressed. For example, when hearing about a poor grade in math, I might say "Isn't it great that Johnny got 80% in his spelling test". Another example could be on hearing about "being really busy," I could say, "Isn't it great that the company closed that deal with xyz the other day?" Even if the other person doesn't hear or take in what I am saying, by using this approach I maintain my positive state of mind. I also feel that I am there for the other person when they are ready to move forward.

When I have someone absorbed in negative behavior that I can't just remove from my life, like a family member, colleague, or important work contact, I need to do what I can to help, but not at the risk of compromising on what I can be. Whether the person is just going through a bad patch or has some clinical issues, I find while useful at times, confronting or ignoring only makes things worse for me, and them. Deliberate positivity on the other hand, has worked to maintain my own positive state and may even help them.

Gratefulness

My favorite trick when it comes to emotions and the mysterious workings of the mind is presented beautifully by Goulston. He suggests that it is impossible to feel gratitude and anger at the same time. Moving myself to a positive and more constructive place on a regular basis is key to engagement with my purpose and my experiences of the world. Therefore, I can reduce anger and other negative emotions simply by being grateful. Additionally, I found that engagement of the gratefulness emotion even gives me a good boost when I am already in a positive place.

Various research studies and books have explored the benefits of gratitude (i.e., Seligman, Steen, Park & Peterson (2005), and Sheldon & Lyubomirsky (2006)). A common theme is the use of a daily reflection of three things to be grateful for. I first explored these techniques with the three-week challenge. This challenge involved a daily capture of three things that I was grateful for. The process involved a daily reminder in my calendar, and a place to write. The process involved writing "I am grateful for," followed by something. I had to write three of these sentences daily for twenty-one days. The research pointed toward having different things each day, but I found that didn't matter as much. The impact on my state of mind was noticeable. During the twenty-one days and for several weeks after, I felt better about myself and more able to face my daily challenges. I repeated the process about six months later and found it had an even bigger impact. Shortly after that, I decided to try it daily. I found the practice set my mind in the right place for the day. After about a year, I changed the start of the sentence to "I am grateful that I am ..." That helped me focus my attention on what I could create. The change in phrase made it more personal, and that helped drive my daily actions even more positively. I now do this every day, at the start of my day, reflecting on the day before. Even during times of trouble and stress, the process brings something good to my thinking as I drive into the unknown. We will explore more uses of gratitude in chapter twenty-one.

Chapter 15: Give and take.

With others, is more fun

I need space on my own for reflection, getting stuff done, and having experiences. Even outside reflective space, I really need to be by myself at times and am no fun to be around. At those times, I am likely to bark if anyone comes near me. On the other hand, I also need shared time. Besides, much of what there is to experience in life is more fun when done with others. It's not always a positive experience, but it is certainly a richer environment for learning and growing, and mostly a lot better than sitting alone on a weekend watching box sets. And finally, my experience of life is greatly enhanced when I give help, advice and pleasure to others, and vice versa. However, there are risks associated with how and how much I give or receive. Too much or too little in either direction can decrease my experience of life and increase my chances of finding myself alone.

I love the concept of Otherish Giving, as outlined by Adam Grant in his 2014 book *Give and Take: Why Helping Others Drives Our Success*. Grant presents case studies and research to show that the majority of those who have had the most success in life, across a range of measures, are givers. Takers don't always make the top of the list as one might expect. Matchers exist in the middle, and there is no surprise there. The startling thing is that while those that give are at the top, they also exist at the bottom. Those that give too much, unconditionally, get taken advantage of and marginalized. Only those that give in a way that stays true to themselves in an uncompromising way, succeed. This alternative approach to giving is what Grant calls "Otherish Giving." It is the idea that we give where it works both for ourselves and others. It's a win-win. It's not the same as matching, which is giving something, and expecting something back of equal or similar quality and quantity. Otherish Giving is unconditional giving, but it's done in a way which allows us to still build and maintain our own physical, mental, and financial wellbeing. It holds true to the notion that to help others we must help ourselves first. We must take that oxygen mask and use it before assisting others. We must take that help or advice when it is offered and use it gratefully without carrying guilt or a feeling of owing. And, we must give back unconditionally but in measures that don't compromise our own wellbeing.

Throughout the various parts of my career, I have had to travel or spend time away from friends and family. That situation created great opportunities to explore the meaning of loneliness. There were lots of times when I relished at the opportunities for interactions with people I had just met or hardly knew. I somewhat became an expert in creating rich interactions with strangers, a skill that has helped me as I moved into coaching, mentoring, and facilitation. However, none of that took away the feeling of what I labeled as loneliness. I found I could mask that feeling with drinking and rich food, which, while helping with socializing, didn't help my mental wellness.

As I started to look deeper at this topic, I learned better ways of understanding the feelings associated with being away from loved ones. Instead of telling myself that I was lonely, I asked myself to think about what I was learning. That shift in perspective enabled me to find specific needs that were absent. The most interesting learning came from an unexpected corner. As I explored learning instead of loneliness, I realized there were aspects of loneliness that even existed when I was with loved ones. Existing in a place of "being lonely" is just too vast to be of any use. Narrowing the focus through a specific line of thought enabled me to look at situations and experiences and understand what I was getting from them or what was lacking.

It is in the social needs

Our social needs are complex, as are the social needs of those in our lives. I need lots of different things. I know that this is true of those I care about and associate with. I need others to be interested in what I am doing (i.e., to listen, to empathize with, and to guide me). I need to be needed (i.e., I need to have opportunities to listen to, to empathize with, and to guide). I need someone to call me out when I am putting myself down, being unrealistic, or simply aiming too high. I need others to care for and to provide for. I need to feel that I am helping in ways that are needed. These needs stretch across a spectrum from intimate/physical, to spiritual, social, and professional. I have physical needs, from the intimate sexual, to hugs with loved ones, to sharing the same physical proximity in social and professional settings. I need to share joy and humor in various forms, from the family-friendly to edgy and adult only. I need to share challenges. I need to share pain and anguish. I need to share excitement and wonder. And, I need to share worthiness.

In exploring my conditioning and breaking down my limiting and borrowed beliefs, one of the most significant discoveries was that my needs can't be satisfied by any single individual. Equally, it's downright limiting to believe that the good that I can bring to the world can be achieved through a couple of associations. I discovered that my needs are complicated and varied, and so too is the network of associations required to meet those needs. My view of what worked was too binary. I broke things down by "personal" and "professional." I came to believe that most of my needs were only met at home and then the remainder were met at work. I even considered the middle ground to be temporary, (i.e., the social aspects associated with friends and family). I believed that once into a relationship, all my non-professional needs would be met there. Boy was I wrong! As well as simply not working, relying on a single person for all my needs was an awful burden to place on them, especially someone I cared about.

I need all kinds of different people in my life if I am truly going to be able to satisfy my social needs. I need dependents, confidants, adversaries, challengers, givers, takers, followers, and role models. I need different things from different people. Those people need different things from me. And what I give to any individual may not necessarily be reciprocated. I may have a friend that often calls for my support, but never offers support back. The mistake in life is to see that as wrong. It simply isn't. It is unrealistic to expect that everyone in my life is in the same place as I am at any given moment. We simply have different types and levels of social needs. An individual relationship may change over time and balance out, but it may not either.

Who will fix my car tire?

Understanding what I need is challenging. Understanding if I am truly having those needs met is a whole different sort of challenge.

Consider the challenge of needing help with a slightly deflated car tire. Being slightly deflated might mean I don't notice it—I might be happily driving around the place unaware that I am putting stress on the tire and increasing the possibility of a more serious problem, like a blow-out. Now consider if someone else notices the deflated car tire. They have a quandary. Do they tell me about it or just ignore it? If they tell me about it, they risk certain things. They risk injuring my ego and being shot down for delivering the message. That might bring them unwanted stress. Alternatively, I might love the drama and invite them to help them fix it. That might get in the way of their plans. If I ask for help, what might that help be? Let's assume I asked for help, either as a result of someone telling me or as a result of me noticing the problem myself. Consider what the possible response might be. Perhaps the other person might offer to use their pump. Perhaps they might even offer to take the car and get it sorted for me. Perhaps the other person might simply give me directions to the nearest place to get the tire inflated. Perhaps the person might take an easier option for them, and simply suggest I abandon the possibility of reflating the tire and suggest I replace it, either with the spare, or by getting someone else to do it. The different types of responses will indicate the different levels of interest in me and my immediate challenge. Now consider if this challenge wasn't a slightly deflated tire. What if the challenge was an unfaithful partner, or a child seen doing something they shouldn't, or a friend speaking behind my back, or a failing business venture, or an unfulfilling job? How would those in my network respond? Would they tell me? What level of support would they give me? Would they help find a solution or would they take an easier path, and suggest I walk away from the challenge?

In understanding how I get my social needs met, I need to avoid having "car insurance companies" in the mix. Not all those in my network have my best interests at heart. I may need them to satisfy my own needs, (i.e., I support them). However, expecting them to reciprocate might bring me more pain. Car insurance companies extract premiums with the promise of support. When something goes wrong, they come to the rescue. However, there is often an excess payment needed before that help comes. Worse still is that when the damage is significant and the possible path to resolution long and hard, they are far too willing to write it off completely. They will offer compensation that is based on the market and often far less than the utility value. Even with cars, this is often unsatisfactory. Consider if the challenge wasn't my car, but my marriage, my parenting, business, or career. Having someone in my network suggest I simply write it off is totally insufficient, and may create far greater challenges.

Groups need people

It sounds obvious, but we often forget the fact that a group needs people. We need more than two people for things to work in a social or professional setting involving a group of people sharing, experiencing, or working together. For most of my life, I have found myself needing to justify my involvement in any group setting. Sure, I appreciated that when it was just me and someone else it was clear there was going to be some give and perhaps take, and that both had a role. However, for groups of three or more, I felt I needed a reason to be there. I felt I needed to have some clear contribution to make or some skill to bring. It never occurred to me that groups need people (i.e., to share ideas or concerns, we need an audience). So, simply being present in the group, at times, might be enough. The right number of people in a group setting increases the value for all involved, even if it's simply just to listen.

While passive involvement in a group setting does work at times, it's not always optimal. When it comes to teams, the interdependency of skills and tasks require active engagement from all those involved. When it works well, the results are spectacular in terms of both outputs and personal growth.

In my mid-twenties, I moved to a new city and went looking for ways to make friends. A business associate was involved in a yacht sailing school and encouraged me to take a course to meet people. I started with a twelve-week course, which I did on Saturdays. At the end of the course I joined a group

127

associated with the school, who met weekly, and participated in short inshore races. We raced 30ft sailing boats in a beautiful protected harbor, so it was hard not to enjoy ourselves. After the racing, we'd gather in a local pub or restaurant for a meal and some wine. I did indeed meet some lifelong friends through that racing, however the learning came a year or so later when I got involved with a more serious racing crew. At the time, I didn't truly understand what I was getting involved in. I signed up because I knew the owner and a couple of others involved and it seemed like a good way to have more fun and on a more regular basis. It was lots of fun as we trained together and then competed in some more serious racing, and eventually the notorious Sydney to Hobart Ocean Race. The learning with respect to groups came with seeing the value individual contributions make to the whole. Sailing with nine others in 10ft waves in gale force winds brings out the best and worst in people. Everyone had a set of skills and a role to play. We all needed to do our tasks properly to compete, and even survive at times. Thankfully, I was blessed, and here to tell the tale. Everyone stepped up and put their best foot forward. Trusting and being part of a team when embracing serious and potentially life-threatening experiences is unbelievably enjoyable and rewarding at the same time. I saw the true value of teamwork when I realized that while crucial to success, my contribution was only a small part. Knowing that I meant something to something important gave me the most incredible feeling of worthiness and purpose. The experience served dual social needs. At the same time, it served my need to give and receive help.

In my mid-teens, my father got hold of a broken-down Austin Champ. This over- engineered British Army jeep from the Second World War, had been used by my uncle as a farm vehicle in the late 1960s and 70s. Over the next two years, with a little help from my father, my brother, a cousin, and a friend, I went about restoring this odd-looking machine. I repaired it mechanically and restored the body work, replaced the army green with jet black paint and turned it into something cool to be seen in. I got it road-worthy and licensed just after my seventeenth birthday. It became my first car. I still remember the looks on my fellow students the day I drove into the high school car park. The crazy-looking black jeep gave me attention like I hadn't known. It gave me the confidence to widen my circle of friends. During that process, I met some of my closest friends to this day. The Austin Champ gave me status and helped bring a new dynamic and strength to the group of friends I became part of. The focal point changed things. Not all those changes were for the good. I lost contact with some of my old friends and things also changed for the group I joined. Not everyone bought into the new context, some moved on. It is clear to me now, that while groups need people, people change groups. My presence in groups or teams has impact and that impact can be both positive and negative. Not all shared experiences will serve me or those that are already in the group before I join. Authenticity in a group setting, therefore, requires that I understand what is important to me and the impact of my presence.

When we show up and get involved, we create wonderful opportunities for growth, both in ourselves, and others, the evidence being in the success of initiatives like Men's Sheds, community groups, workplace wellbeing committees as well as the traditional team sports. Having a clear understanding of why we are involved in something is important, because, as I discovered, at times it's not clear at the offset what the impact of shared experiences will have on the wellbeing of us and others.

That one special person

The most frightening and revealing learning to date has been seeing the burden I was carrying with respect to the one love, that one person that meant the world to me. Love is such a confusing concept. I count myself very lucky as I've experienced lots of love. I have been loved as a son, brother, grandson, nephew, cousin, friend, lover, husband, father, colleague, team member, leader, coach, motivator, and facilitator. And yes, I count myself very lucky because I've had opportunities to love. However, is being loved or sharing love, the same as being "in love?" Or, is there a difference between loving something about another or simply "loving" them. And more importantly, does it really matter? Isn't "in love" really about infatuation? Doesn't it fuel the honeymoon stage of a relationship? Also, isn't "loving someone" simply about caring unconditionally? So, what's all the fuss about?

Does "in love" automatically translate to being loved or being able to love? It doesn't. However, that's not necessarily a bad thing. To be loved or to love is context -specific and doesn't need to be all-encompassing. Sure, we need high levels of trust for love to work properly, however that trust only needs to extend as far as the context requires it. For example, being loved by a parent requires a level of trust that is not the same as being loved by a lover. The types of honesty required in those situations isn't the same.

Love is just another need, be it a quite complicated one. How we realize love depends on the context and that can vary. My mistake was to believe all my love needs could be obtained from one individual. Holding onto this belief got in the way of building strong relationships or getting out of bad ones. I am not saying that I satisfy the same need via multiple different people. While I can get the same type of love I need as a son from both parents, or as a brother from multiple siblings or a leader from thousands of followers, there are certain types of love, specifically the intimate kind, which might be best sourced from a single individual. The trick is to narrow down the specific needs from each person in my life and not overly burden one individual with more than is reasonable to expect of them.

Trust

Trust is crucial to relationships. Behaviors that build trust include a 100% commitment to sharing feelings, both positive, and negative. Behaviors that build trust include acknowledging my desires (i.e., talking openly about what I need, what isn't being met, and being honest when I am attracted to, or aroused by, someone outside the relationship). Having desires that aren't agreeable within the relationship or being attracted to someone else doesn't automatically lead to infidelity, or even the demise of the relationship. I am kidding myself if I claim I have never been attracted to or been aroused by someone else while already in a relationship. It's the lack of honesty that causes me grief. Instead of being honest with my partner, I feel guilty. I feel I have done something wrong, simply because my natural desires were aroused by someone else. Getting berated by my partner for sharing my desires, no matter where they came from, isn't about me, it's about them. It is a signal that they have baggage, be it a self-image problem or some deeper psychological issues. It is totally unrealistic and a perfect reason to visit some hard questions about the nature of the relationship. Behaviors that build trust include being honest about all the aspects, including what excites me, what scares me, and what's in the way. Behaviors that build trust include assuming the right intent, always.

Building trust and therefore the ability to love, starts with trust. That sounds like a chicken and egg conversation, and that's because it is. Trust doesn't start with distrust. Trust starts with trust. Starting from a position of trust requires courage and, fundamentally, belief in ourselves. For example, and as touched on in chapter thirteen, think about the last time you said or heard "What are you thinking?" For the person asking the question, why did they ask that question? Is something worrying them about the other person? Did the other person do or say something that confuses them? Does the way they look imply that something needs to be talked about? Or is the person doing the asking really trying to distract themselves from their own thoughts? Perhaps the person doing the asking is hiding something and doesn't want to talk about it. Perhaps the person doing the asking is just bored and doesn't want to own up to that. What about the person being asked? What happens to them when they receive this question? When I try to second guess what another is feeling or thinking, I invite suspicion. When I share that I am worried or scared, I invite trust.

Growing together (or not)

Relationships are not straightforward, emotional and physically intimate ones being the most complex. As already explored in chapter three, traction in starting relationships is greatly aided by dropping the barriers and then allowing ourselves to experience vulnerability. From that place we can learn and grow. It's that aspect that allows the strongest bonds to be built. Learning and growing together creates shared experiences. These shared experiences can be joyous and painful. Either way they are shared, and that can have its advantages. Looking back at ourselves and laughing, or crying, is the fuel that helps us move through and beyond the daily grind. And, doing that with someone who shares those lessons, or at least can relate to them, is nothing short of magical. It is for this reason that I now choose carefully when building trust with new people. I really can't be bothered anymore engaging with someone that doesn't want to see their experiences as opportunities for learning. I give a wide birth to anyone that claims they have all the answers or have no problems. Everyone has baggage and things to learn. For those who accept they don't have their stuff together, they are lucky, because through acceptance, they are already 80% there to getting their stuff together. It is those that are in denial that really need attention. These people will find themselves without a spear and face-to-face with a vicious carnivore, or in the path of a fast-moving bus. I certainly don't want to be anywhere near them when it all goes horribly wrong.

They say, "A problem shared is a problem halved". This is all well and good in theory. Just consider if a single person was the recipient of the "halves," for all my problems or even worse, for everyone they know. Those "halves" would soon add up to a lot of "wholes." That's too much for anyone to shoulder. Coming home after a hard day and offloading the day's challenges on my partner is easy and gives me relief. But at what cost? If I did that day after day, things aren't going to end well! The weight of the difficult stuff I endure is better shared around. Perhaps there are some aspects of my challenging experiences that can be shared with a colleague or friend, before I get home. Spreading the burden of my woes, has the same benefit for my own mental wellbeing, and it reduces the load on that someone special in my life. The same goes for individual friends or family members. I don't want to be bottling up all my worries and concerns and carrying them around with me only to then dump them on family members when I find myself with them, drinking white wine in the sun at Christmas time. Sharing all my baggage in one big offload is too much for the best of us to endure.

Helping others helps me in many ways. Least of all it helps me build my own skill in observing and managing my own emotions. However, helping others is not straightforward. This is especially challenging when the ego is driving my thinking (more on that topic in chapter twenty-one). If I feel someone near me needs help, I find the best thing to do is to ask them. I might simply say to them

"Are you okay?" Assuming they say "No," I simply then ask them how I may help them. Perhaps I might say, "Oh, I am sorry to hear that. What would help you right now?" The key is to make it about them, not me. I then need to be open to what comes back and be prepared to go out of my way to help. If what they ask of me is something that compromises who I am, I need to tell them exactly that. For example, I might respond with "I don't feel comfortable doing that; it doesn't agree with what I feel is right for me." Silence is also very useful here as it might help them rationalize the situation and suggest something else. Not doing what they ask for any other reason, even if I feel it isn't in their interest, is my values and beliefs speaking, not theirs. That also applies to suggesting something they didn't ask for. It's likely just going to annoy them and push them away. If I get a "Yes, everything is okay," and I feel that isn't the case, I try to give them space. The amount of space will be very specific to the situation—it could be minutes, hours, days, weeks, or even months. However, I don't like to turn away if I have strong concerns. I know I should revisit the same questions at an appropriate time. An alternative could be to approach someone that also knows this person and let them know I am concerned. When sharing with another, I wouldn't elaborate too much as it risks bringing my judgment into the situation. That could be counterproductive. I'd simply say, "I have a feeling ___ isn't okay," and leave it at just "a feeling." I wouldn't even suggest any action. I'd leave that to the other person to initiate.

Not all relationships will serve me. There are big advantages in being there to help others, as there is in allowing others to help me. I need to give in order to receive. And I need to give others the opportunity to do the same. However, there is a difference between someone genuinely needing help and someone simply being needy. When I find myself the constant recipient of offloading with little opportunity for my own personal growth, I need to be honest with myself. It is hard to say no when someone is in need. It is hard to say, "no, actually my needs come first." Unfortunately, I must be brave. That hard choice is in my best interests, as well as theirs. Toxic people and their behaviors have no place in my life. They can devastate my experience and wellbeing. For example, there is no place for someone who says something toxic quietly to make me angry, then says something trivial and unrelated out loud to attract attention, thus giving the impression that I am angry and unreasonable to anyone else in the room. There is no place for behaviors involving manipulation, seeking admiration and special treatment, or that are callous and insensitive. Choosing who I learn and grow with takes investment, and vigilance. I must be flexible, willing to change who I invite into my life.

The investment

As someone who has been married and then gone back into the dating world, I have concluded that there are many people, single or in a relationship, who have found comfort in a somewhat mediocre and less than fulfilling existence. They have their work and their distractions, and between all that, they get by. It's far easier to give in than to confront an unsatisfactory relationship or put themselves out there to meet someone else. As mentioned in chapter three, making changes to their context is just too much of a stretch. They are unwilling to spend less time with some of their friends or family, to make room to engage or reengage with the other person. They are unwilling to change some of their routines and habits to fit better with the availability of the other. They are unwilling to work on their physical condition so that they can have better physical engagement. They are unwilling to seek help to remove more of the baggage. They are unwilling to reduce their financial security somewhat, so they have the means to engage fully in new and shared experiences. Good things take investment and maintenance, and quality relationships are no exception.

There is an extension to the Doorstep concept we explored in chapter seven. The idea is that once I get over the need to present a rose-colored view of myself, I start to let people in. The "Door" (or hall), "Lounge" and "Kitchen" work well to explain the stages I go through. So, let's picture someone calling to my door. If I don't know or trust them, I am unlikely to let them over the doorstep. Depending on my home configuration and the weather, I may let them into the hall, but only just, and with the door left open. The conversation happens and ends there. Now, consider they call again. Perhaps I now know more about them. Perhaps I asked around and have some level of respect for them or I like them. But I don't trust them yet. So, now I bring them into the lounge, or "Good Room." I might offer them coffee, tea, biscuits, and cake. This space is somewhat staged and presents my best self. I keep this space tidy and it doesn't give too much away about the way I live and who I am. The conversations now take a slightly richer color but are not fully open. Let's move forward. So, I've enjoyed multiple conversations in the lounge and the trust has built up to a good level. This is the point they get invited to sit at the kitchen table. From the kitchen table they get to see the real me. They get to see the disarray, the worn surfaces, and chipped cups. They get to see how I live my life and who I am. It's not realistic that everyone I know will sit at my kitchen table, nor do I want that. There are plenty of associations that will work perfectly from the doorstep. There are many that will serve my and their needs, simply in the lounge. However, to build the network of associations required to meet my social needs, I must let the right people sit at my kitchen table. That will take time and effort to know who is truly worthy.

All good things take big investment and ongoing maintenance. Building meaningful and purposeful social, intimate, and professional relationships is no different. The effort needed should not be overlooked or taken for granted. It's unrealistic to think it will just happen. It takes effort, and not just upfront. It takes effort over the course of the relationship. It's not like winning the lotto (i.e., a small investment with big returns), which is fun to play but takes little or no effort. Things get tough over the course of a relationship. The storms that we face will put pressure into places we don't expect: the economic downturns, personal injury or ill-health, the sudden illness or death of loved ones, and the environmental impact. It is unrealistic to expect not to see these in my journey. If I have under-invested, it is during these tough times that the cracks will widen and I risk sinking. Equally, too much focus on the long-term play is just as limiting. I am going to struggle to have an engaging experience if I only put a penny in each month. Very little will come of that until perhaps when I am in my 70s, retired, looking at buying a new suit for my neighbor's funeral. It might work for superficial "Doorstep" acquaintances, but not for rewarding long-term "kitchen table" relationships. Life is to be lived today, not tomorrow. I need to invest big at the offset and be willing to continue to put more in over the course of time.

The Social Needs Relationship Matrix

Reward is not without risk. It's an old saying and it is so true, and it applies to investing the time and effort in building relationships to meet my social needs. It is hard at the start of a new association to be completely open. Perhaps I fear that I'll be taken advantage of or hurt. Perhaps I fear the effort will be wasted if things don't go the distance. I allow those fears to hold me back. That is the mistake. I carry fears of one-night-stands or getting to know the new neighbor, part-time or casual labor colleagues because there's no guarantee I will be seeing or working with them again tomorrow. However, there is a middle ground. The middle ground is being clear about who I am, being realistically optimistic, being clear about what I need, and allowing myself to give and to receive. We will explore more of bringing all that together in chapter nineteen, for now let's focus on the social needs and build from there.

The Social Needs Relationship Matrix is a tool I use to assess whether my social needs are or are not being met by those in my world. The tool helps me see where I need to focus effort, both from an initial investment and maintenance viewpoint. It gives a very clear line of sight. The steps are as follows:

1. I open a spreadsheet, or I could have used a piece of graph paper.

2. In the first column, down the page, I list my social needs, putting one need per row.

   In exploring my social needs, I look at what I need in terms of giving and receiving. I also look at aspects of my personal and professional experience. If I get stuck, I think about the interactions I have had with others. I consider what topics were part of those interactions. I consider who was doing the talking and who was doing the listening. I look for experiences with others where I felt high levels of emotions, both positive and negative. I describe the opportunities for giving and receiving separately. I am very specific when I know there is an interaction that I need from one individual and I am more general when a group of people are involved.

   Here are some examples:

Support me in my physical wellbeing

Support others in their physical wellbeing

Support me in building better habits

Support others in building better habits

Listen to/empathize with my ideas of intimacy

Guide me in my ideas of intimacy

Listen to/empathize with my ideas on building friendship

Guide me in my ideas of building friendships

Listen to/empathize with my personal development ideas

Guide me in my personal development

Listen to/empathize with my professional development ideas

Guide me in my professional development

Listen to/empathize with my spirituality related notions

Guide me in my spirituality

Listen to/empathize with other's ideas of intimacy

Guide others in their ideas of intimacy

Listen to/empathize with others in their personal endeavors

Guide others in their personal endeavors

Listen to/empathize with others in their professional endeavors

Guide others in their professional endeavors

Sexual Intimacy

Hugs

Play

Physical proximity

Call me out for putting myself down.

Call me out for being unrealistic/aiming too high.

Care for/provide for

Share joy/humor—family

Share joy/humor—adult

Share value creation

Share growing (pain/anguish)

Share excitement/wonder

Share worthiness

3. In each of the column headings, I write the name of key people or groups of people in my life. For example, I wrote my partner's name in column two, the names of each of my children in columns three to seven, the names of my parents and siblings in the next set of columns, and then my business partners, followed by the names of my close friends. I then put "coaching clients," "workshop participants," "followers" and my various groups, communities, and professional associations in separate column headings after that. And, finally, I listed my support network (i.e., my doctor, physiotherapist, coach, trainer etc).

4. Now I review each cell and give it a number, if appropriate. I either leave it blank, or give it a one, two, or three. I would leave the cell blank if that person or group of people had no impact whatsoever on the social need. I would give the cell a one or a two if the person or group occasionally help

meet that social need. I give one if there is a good bit of effort required on my part (i.e., if I must go out of my way to bring this person into my life to help with the related social need), otherwise I would give a two. I would give a three when that person regularly helps me with that social need.

The results would look something like the following:

Need \ Person	Partner	Son 1	Son 2	Colleague	Client	Doctor
Support me in my physical wellbeing	2					1
Hugs	3	2	2		1	
Listen to / Empathize with my professional development ideas	1			1		
Guide others in their professional endeavors	1			1	3	

5. With the scores in place, I add them up, and look for patterns. I know there is a need for investment when across my existing connections, I'm not getting at least three in total (i.e., in the example above "Listen to/empathize with my professional development ideas" isn't being met). Perhaps I need to take action to address that? Secondly, I look for big winners (i.e., "Partner" in this example has the highest score). If I am to maintain the current level of wellbeing, I had better invest effort to make sure that relationship is well-maintained.

To work on the patterns, I find it useful to print the spreadsheet. I could also make a photocopy of a hand drawn chart. I can then write my action plan directly against the needs and individuals I want to focus on. Later, I will revisit that piece of paper to reflect on my progress.

The patterns I see in this chart will be relevant for where I am now. Over time, these will change as I change, and as people come into and out of my life. I revisit this matrix as I need to (i.e., when I meet new people, lose contact, or something major shifts in an existing relationship).

The matrix provides useful information in helping me manage my network of friends,, family, and peers. In having my social needs met, it will show me where I need to invest and maintain. It will also show me where I have risks. It's worth considering action if I see a single individual scoring two or three times higher than anyone else. Not only does it show that the individual has a lot to shoulder, but it shows me to be in a vulnerable position should that individual no longer be part of my experience. That could be because of a breakup or falling out. It could simply be because I change my context and they aren't as available anymore. It could also be because of something more painful, like death, or someone becoming mentally incapacitated. The pain and ability to bounce forward after a significant loss is going to be considerably more difficult if that departed individual was also a key part of my support network. There is a lot of merit in widening my network through rekindling old friendships and repairing bridges, especially as I get older. I am not saying I shouldn't expect to have anyone in my experience that I rely on and will miss dearly, that is not realistic. I should just be mindful of how much I focus on one individual and have some alternatives available. It is simply important to have the support around me when I need it.

Chapter 16: Bringing my body with me.

Being normal?

There is nothing straightforward to keeping in shape and maintaining adequate energy levels, especially when we are fast approaching, or beyond, mid-life. Things start to creak, get wobbly, greyer, and less responsive. The busyness has us drained by late afternoon. Even those who in their earlier years could eat what they like, do very little exercise, and still bounce through their day with vigor and enthusiasm, will eventually find themselves lethargic, inflexible and being a whole lot more buoyant than they'd like. Sorry for being the bearer of bad news and the killjoy. I'm not sorry really, as I'm there too! Besides, you already knew it, either personally, or through someone you know.

For much of my teenage and early adult life, I perceived myself as a little chubby. The self-perception made me self-conscious of how I looked. For a time, I had the belief that I wasn't liked very much because of my chubbiness. It probably was a factor, however it never occurred to me that my personality and how I behaved around others was also a significant aspect. I got stuck on the belief that, if I just got a little less chubby, all my problems would be solved. I was right and wrong at the same time. The self-image impacted how I behaved. I was wrong in that people aren't all that shallow. I was right in that if I shifted my perceptions, things changed. A shift in self-image impacted how I behaved around others and it impacted my attitude toward exercise, food, and drink. Over time I also learned there was more to it all than just exercise, food, and drink. I came to appreciate it was a full package that included mental wellness and sleep. I learned that to have the energy and confidence to engage fully with work and play, I had to give focus to what I did with my body.

Sweating

Somewhere along my journey I got it into my head that I wasn't a runner, which is still a mystery to me as I have photos of me at age ten on the podium in first place at school running events. And yet, I stopped. In my teens I did team sports and surfing, but no running. In my twenties I took up inline skates, which

141

I enjoyed, but still no running. I tried to go walking regularly in my thirties and yet I was afraid of lifting the legs that little bit further.

Running didn't return to my journey until I was into my early forties. I had enough of being low on energy and not being able to keep up with my kids at the playground or the pitch. Something had to change. The timing coincided with my journey to shedding limiting and borrowed beliefs. However, getting to a place where running was part of my regular routine didn't happen overnight. In fact, it took nearly three years. My first attempt lasted four weeks. I set myself a target of achieving thirty minutes of jogging. I did a combination of walking and jogging, increasing the time from fifteen minutes initially, adding minutes each day. I gave up once I reached thirty minutes. I had met my goal. It took nearly another twelve months before I tried again. I decided I needed to raise the bar. I decided I needed to be able to run 5K in good time. Over the course of the next eighteen months I built it up to running almost daily. I ran thirty to forty-five minutes to the point where I was daily running 5K. There were some gaps, of a week, or so at times, when I didn't do any running, but only in the first six months. From there running regularly became a normal part of my experience. I know all of this because I measured it. I constructed a chart where I would give myself a daily score on my progress. I would give myself a score of between zero and three, where a score of zero meant that I didn't attempt; a score of one meant I did attempt but didn't finish it; two meant that I ran for at least fifteen minutes of the session; and three meant I ran the full thirty minutes. At the end of those first six months it was clear something was missing. I was not sufficiently motivated, and I was being too hard on myself. I wasn't being realistic. So, I adjusted the scoring system. I added to the score of "one" the idea of other light exercise,, like sit-ups, gardening, a family walk, or kicking a ball with my kids. I added to the score of "two" other types of exercise, like a family bike-ride or a good session of strength building. Eventually I didn't need the chart. However, to maintain the regular 5K run, I needed something else. Raising the bar helped, however I needed better reasons to continue. I needed better motivation.. I will return to motivation later in the chapter.

Yoga is not for blokes. "Bloke" is slang, used regularly in Australia where I grew up. It's often associated with "good bloke," which refers to someone of good standing who does the right thing. For me the term also represents masculinity. I first tried yoga in my thirties, before the busyness of raising children. I went along because my wife was interested, and I figured it was a gateway to better engagement. I gave it my best shot, but eventually gave up, after two years. I got tired of feeling uncomfortable and struggling to breathe with my oversized belly squashing down on me during shoulder stands. The better engagement didn't materialize either. The yoga simply put us in a room of more flexible and able people, and mostly women. It took more time out of our week and the opportunity for time together. I firmly filed the experience as something for someone else, and certainly not for blokes.

Fast forward fourteen years and I was in a different place, but still not convinced of the benefits of yoga. I was even a coach by this stage and actively exploring mindfulness and other forms of disconnecting and reflection. Additionally, I was running regularly, and keen to diversify my exercise. I was learning about the importance of variety in keeping the momentum. And, I was keen to do things that put me in contact with different circles as I rebuilt my social network following the demise of my marriage. But I was still unsure of what role yoga played. I was at a networking event, talking with a group. We were talking about regular exercise. I shared that I enjoyed running, but that I was often in pain. We spoke about building core strength and how it helped prevent injury and pain. I asked about any ideas for building core strengths and someone suggested Bikram Yoga.. She described it as a 90-minute session in a very hot room with lots of other sweaty bodies doing yoga. It sounded odd to me. Then she mentioned that she had seen some of our provincial rugby team players in the sessions. The mention of rugby players had me interested. They were blokes, and some of the toughest. I was also intrigued by the potential for increasing the opportunity for dating again.

It took me another six months before I finally found myself in the hot room. I had to get past my beliefs around yoga. I also had come across some negative press about the founder of Bikram Yoga. Once I put all that to bed, I took a risk, and gave it a try, and boy, was I in for some eating humble pie. As an aside, it

143

was not as good as I thought it would be for meeting women. The room was at best 50% women and any of the limited socializing was confined to the change rooms before or after sessions. However, it was good because of three other aspects. Firstly, Bikram Yoga is largely stretching, and balancing postures aimed at core strengths instead of traditional yoga postures. So, there were no suffocating shoulder stands. Secondly, it is done in an incredibly hot room, making it easier to work the various core strength muscle groups. Finally, the heat and intensity of the sessions leaves no space for preoccupation with what others think or the woes of the day. The mind is forced to let go and focus only on the breathing and next posture. It is a forced form of mindfulness. These sessions aren't a walk in the park, however the feeling of wellbeing, both physical, and emotional, when the session is completed, is stupendous. And, I learned that yoga can be for blokes too.

My final piece of learning brings realistic optimism back into the picture. Moving my body to do things it hadn't ever done, or hadn't done for a good stretch, had its complications. As I got more into running, bike riding, walking, and Bikram Yoga, I broke things. I found that the years of neglect had caused things to tighten to the point of snapping. So, the progress toward a better physical me needed help. That help came in the form of regular sessions with a chartered physiotherapist. Getting the right balance of exercise into busy lives is far from simplistic. It takes trial and error to find the right type and frequency that suits our own journey, and not someone else's.

Fuel and poison

Food and drink have always been a reward. I grew up with icons of men having beers after a hard day's work. Lavish dinners are commonplace when a goal or milestone is realized. I still see now in my community with my kids, success in a match being immediately celebrated with cakes and treats, or an outing to McDonalds. Tasty food and drinks definitely add to the sense of enjoyment associated with the success or achievement. The rich food and drinks are associated with good times. I am not in wonder, therefore, as to why I reach for a snack, usually something high in salt, sugar, or fat, when I am feeling both disappointed and excited. The conditioning is just too strong.

144

When I am feeling like something is just too hard or I get a knock back, the desire to stuff my face with sugary, salty and fatty foods, or crack open a beer or bottle of wine, is very strong. This is the need to return to that happy place where rich food and drink is plentiful, which is totally counterproductive. When things are hard and the mind is overworking the fears, loading up with food and drink that take effort to process and do little to fuel my body, is the worst thing to do. This fact is very real to me, yet, I still choose to ignore it.

Let's be very honest, there is no magic wand on this. There is no straightforward set of steps. No one single solution that works unilaterally. However, there are a few things that I have found useful. This includes reading labeling to understand the contents, getting more fiber and protein so I have more energy, drinking lots of water, and using anchoring to build new habits, the most successful of those anchoring processes being when I introduced, "I don't need this; I don't want this." I anchored this chant to my arm reaching toward a salty, fatty, or sugary snack. It works in part, but only when I am already in a positive place.

Without a doubt, the most significant thing that helped move my eating and drinking habits in a positive direction was reversing the conditioning relating to reward. I now look at food and drink as fuel to obtain reward, not the reward itself. For example, try losing the mantra that says, "If I do this now, I can reward myself with that slice of cake." Replace it with, "I'll have this slice of cake now because I am heading out for a walk and will use the excess sugars." By seeing energy as the reward of food and drink, I started making better arrangements ahead of time. I started stocking the fridge and cupboard with ingredients for more healthy eating. I started planning my meals and snacks based on what I was doing and the associated energy needs. For example, I don't need the same types and quantity of food if I am sitting at my desk all day, verses spending a day on my feet in a workshop or running around the place taking kids to matches and engaging with them.

Seeing food and drink as the fuel to obtain reward also allowed me to let go of the associated guilt. I chose to eat and drink because I needed to, or wanted to, but not as the reward for using energy. As a result, I found myself getting even more enjoyment out of eating and drinking. Seeing food and drink as fuel, not reward, helped me feel better about myself. From there I made even better choices about not only what went into my body, but what I did with my body as well. This revelation became the catalyst for the title of this book. Choosing to eat something loaded with sugars and fat, like fried chicken, doesn't make me a bad person. It doesn't compromise who I am. It is simply eating something that needs more focus so that I burn off the resulting sugar, fat, and toxins. Enjoying something in the right quantities is the key. That doesn't mean I haven't overindulged on a bucket of chicken, and it doesn't mean I still won't. It simply means that I accept that it is my choice and that it is on me to manage the consequences.

Recovery

I love sleep. The softness of the bed and the feeling of pulling up the duvet is so special after a long and busy day. I love the "roll-over," when you wake and then realize that there is another hour left before you need to really get up. I love sleep now, because I sleep well. I rarely toss and turn. I am usually asleep within minutes of my head hitting the pillow, and I sleep deeply, and typically feel very refreshed when I wake. But that wasn't always the case. I would struggle getting to sleep and wake often during the night. Other than alcohol-fueled stupors, sleep was a disjointed, and sometimes seemingly unattainable prize.

Regularly getting better sleep took effort and focus. However, the biggest hurdle was a limiting belief. I had become aligned with the idea of "there will be plenty of time for sleep when you are six feet under pushing up daisies." I had aligned with the idea that to get more done and engage with life better, you needed to be awake more. I believed that sleep was for amateurs—for lazy people who wouldn't amount to much. I remember a story of the owner of a company I contracted through at one stage in my twenties. He boasted about only getting four hours sleep. He was minted and appeared to have a fabulous life. Perhaps it works for some, however it definitely didn't work for me. The poor sleep left me unable to engage fully with my work. The tiredness had me reaching for comfort food and alcohol as the norm, not the exception.

It became a cycle of poor sleep leading to even less sleep as I entertained my seemingly awake mind with late night TV, alcohol, and more snacks.

The benefits of quality sleep are well documented. DNA research even points to sleep being necessary for the brain to repair. It appears that during our awake periods, strands of our DNA break as we engage our cognitive functions. We self-repair these strands, but when we are awake the repair process falls behind. It only catches up when we switch off completely. If we don't give our brain time to recover, we stop. After a time, we need to shut down and recharge. The best way to experience this is to fly from London to Sydney and drink and watch movies the whole way. On the ground, and after the excitement of seeing old friends and family wears off, things get wobbly. As the fatigue takes over, we go through stages of annoyance, then anger, and then confusion. At some point after that, we will get completely zombie-like. We won't be able to think, and our body will simply stop functioning. When having babies, the first nine to twelve weeks produces similar results for new parents. Another way to think of this is like dirty dishes. If we simply stack the dishes and keep making new meals without washing up, eventually there will be either no dishes to use or no space to cook, or both. The kitchen becomes unusable. This is where the DNA research is pointing.

The process of getting better sleep is also well researched. We now know improving sleep requires attention to what we eat and when we eat I (i.e., avoiding large meals in the evening). We know drinking water to be hydrated properly helps. We know the quantity of caffeine intake impacts the quality of sleep. We know that we should reduce alcohol and avoid it one hour or two before hitting the pillow. We know how blue light, from phones and computers, impacts our brain patterns, and that gets in the way of our brain moving into a recovery phase. We know how keeping a pen and paper beside us at night helps to let go if we wake with something on our mind. We also know that sex, regular exercise and therefore fitness, enables us to sleep better. We know we can catch up on sleep during the day, when managed in the right quantities and right time of the day. There is also lots of research done into variable heart rate and how understanding the patterns gives us

147

insight into where things are working and where they are not. We know lots about what helps us obtain better quality sleep.

However, bringing all that together is easier said than done. It's a chicken and egg conversation. If I am not thinking properly or I have little energy, I am less likely to make better choices. I am less likely to eat well, exercise, reduce alcohol, turn off the TV, or avoid using devices in the late hours. It's simply unrealistic. I need to get better quality sleep and give my brain the space to repair, before I am more likely to make the changes that bring about better quality sleep. It's a circular argument. So that wasn't working for me. Even after I found ways to clear my mind completely of all my concerns and commitments, as I'll share in chapter twenty, I still wasn't getting quality sleep. The thing that made the difference was learning a technique that enabled me to get to sleep in an instant. Having the ability to fall into deep sleep on demand increased the likelihood that I'd get more sleep. More sleep enabled more repair. More repair enabled better cognitive capacity during the day. That led to better decisions. That led to changes in behavior and that led to better quality sleep.

The technique that I use to get to sleep instantly is simply to stop thinking. That sounds obvious and might be straightforward for some. However, it wasn't for me. As well as a constant thinker, I love to daydream. Hitting the pillow was an opportunity to work through what happen during the day and to visualize where I was going. It was an opportunity for fantasizing about all kinds of wonderful things I could do or places I could be. I enjoyed it, but it kept me awake. I had to stop. So, I started exploring mindfulness techniques. I was already getting well practiced at letting go of my thoughts, pushing them away from my conscious mind. That helped but still involved me actively thinking. The mindfulness process was still new to me and took effort. So, that wasn't the answer, yet. Then, I came across an idea about focusing the eyes. I can't remember where; it was well before I thought I'd ever be writing about it, so I didn't write down the reference. The technique involves looking at the inside of my eye lids, acknowledging the colors slightly, and then bringing the focus together. It is almost like crossing the eyes when making funny faces as a kid, but not to that point of it being painful. Repeating that slowly four or five times is generally enough, as far as I can tell because I usually don't remember much after that and wake up some time later. Over time, I found I could also use mindfulness to bring sleep on quickly, however the fall back is still the eye technique. This is especially true if I am overtired, preoccupied, or want to take a twenty-minute power nap. With better quality sleep, came better quality decisions, and that is where the truth to recovery rests.

Motivation

After years of procrastinating about it, I eventually found a means to take regular exercise. I had developed beliefs that I couldn't do it. While never confirmed, I suspect I borrowed it from the generation before me. It became clear to me that I fall short of how I teach others because I rely on my own context not theirs. I found myself doing the same thing with my son, and it was then that I saw my behavior in motion. Through school I was told that I needed to practice more, and I carried guilt about that, because I didn't. Here is the thing. I didn't want to practice more. I would do the training; I got a turn on the pitch (mostly) and that was it. I didn't have enough reason to engage with it more than I did. I can't really remember why I even joined those sports. I think it was because I wanted to make friends, and that failed because the "reserve guy" isn't anyone's friend. Perhaps I just did it because that is what I thought people did. I was much happier drawing or creating things with Lego. I lacked the motivation to practice more. Failure to practice held me back. It reduced the participation and the potential for growth and learning.

After finishing school, I did some other team sports, I did ocean racing, spent time going to a gym, took up rollerblading, and tried power walking. None of these worked and I didn't continue doing them, i.e., I lost interest, the activity wasn't realistic given my circumstances or didn't deliver enough benefits in terms of health and fitness. While I enjoyed the feeling of being involved and being active, nothing seemed to stick.

As an example, during the early stages of taking up running, I believed I needed to keep myself busy while running, so I got a tablet and set it up to watch box sets while I used a treadmill. What I found was that the technology often let me down, and I loved the excuse to spend time fixing that instead of exercising. In the second attempt I started running outside as the weather was more suitable, but I still failed to get the exercise to the level I wanted it to be at.

The thing that changed everything was when I started aligning the exercise with other goals I was striving for. I found that the time spent running ticked other boxes. It was time to myself, it was time to think, it was time to be mindful, and it got me away from snacking. In addition, I found ways to efficiently capture my thoughts as I ran. I built in time within my day to extract the recordings. The daily exercise became the place where I reflected and generated more ideas than any other part of my day. Once I had the other benefits identified and understood, it was much easier to haul myself out of bed on cold and dark mornings and get going with my exercise routine. At times I'd run on the treadmill and other times, out on the roads. Over time it became easier and easier to get out the door, even in bad weather. I had found multiple reasons to undertake the running. The same has been applied to other types of exercise. Bike riding is quality time with my kids. Bikram Yoga is forced quiet time. Hill walking creates reflective space.

My experience with exercise can be mirrored with sleep and eating. The motivation to apply myself is multifaceted. Practicing a new behavior or shedding a firm limiting belief is much easier when there are overlapping reasons. These crossed-over motivations reduce the chances of compromise when one aspect is achieved or not relevant anymore.

Being someone who is intrinsically motivated I know all too well how my own thoughts get in the way of self-improvement. While I enjoy it, I don't need approval from others to know I am doing a good job. I measure myself on how well I apply myself. I am driven by the internal rewards of simply doing it. I orient toward the good feelings associated with something, especially where it avoids pain. Unfortunately, this trait is completely useless the moment I self-rationalize my action or inaction. Getting out for a run or not snacking takes an incredible amount of willpower when it is just me and my self-talk. For those that are extrinsically motivated having a reward to look forward to is a significant driver of behavior. Not so much for the likes of me. I don't need to compete in a community 5K run and get a good time, to know I can run 5K well. Nor do I need to get top marks in an exam to know I understand the material. However, I have found that aligning myself with some sort of external accountability does help. By that, I mean sharing what I am doing with others who I care about and I know care about me. I found that the process of sharing makes me more likely to stay committed to a new behavior, be it running regularly, having a smaller meal, or leaving the packet of biscuits unopened. I found the audience was important. Sharing that I am working on a new desired behavior with my network as a broadcast didn't really help. Sharing with those close to me did. It was the level of importance that I placed on my relationship with the other person, that mattered, not that they knew. Being intrinsically motivated meant I had to live up to the standards I set for myself, which included not letting others down. I felt accountable to honoring the promise I had made to myself in their presence. The process of identifying who are the right folks to involve is as explored in chapter fifteen. Inclusion of my physical wellbeing in the Social Needs Relationship Matrix was key to ensuring I was motivated appropriately.

Results?

The process of bringing my body with me had some unexpected benefits. The increase in fitness and energy levels helped in places that I expected. It resulted in delivering a clearer mind, keeping up with the kids at the pitch, not feeling tired, making better eating and drinking choices, and having much better sex. However, it was another aspect that surprised me. As I clocked up the years and added the weight, hangovers got increasingly challenging. I was even drinking less than the crazy years as a young adult. The pain and disruption to my ability to be a good father, husband, son, friend etc., was getting harder and harder even after a modest night of merriment. The surprise for me was the positive impact the fitness had on hangovers. It reversed the trend. The clearer priorities helped me drink more water during and immediately following drinking. The fitness helped my body process the alcohol faster. All of that helped reduce the negative impact of the socializing. Sure, I still need to force myself out of bed to exercise and run regularly, even after a big night. However, that process of getting the blood flowing and enriched with oxygen helps clear the head, and that makes for better eating choices. The better eating and drinking choices alone speed up the process of returning to full potential after a night of self-poisoning.

Bringing my body with me is a journey, not an end point. It isn't something that I do just today and not tomorrow. Attention to what I put in and what I do with my body is the key to physical wellbeing. With physical wellbeing I think clearer, and I engage more with every interaction and activity. All that gives me a better experience of the world.

PART 4:
MOMENTUM

Chapter 17: It is not that hard?

Hard work

For me, "hard" relates to something that I am reluctant to do. When I want or must focus my attention in a certain direction, what does the use of the word "hard" do to my engagement and willingness? As I explored this question, it became clear that I needed to find an alternative that motivated me toward where I wanted to go, and not away from it. If we look at the definition of "hard" we get something like "solid, rigid or not easily broken," as well as "something needing a great deal of effort." I was using the word "hard" to mean that I needed to apply effort or focus. This was because there was some resistance in me or in others involved in what I needed to get done. It wasn't that I was trying to break through a wall or break blocks of wood with my bare hands. There were just obstacles that needed to be moved or avoided to get stuff done. I already firmly believed I could find a way if I set my mind to it. However, by using the word "hard" when I spoke with others, I gave them the impression that I thought something was impossible, when I was just talking about something as having a tolerable level of resistance. From this I learned that I needed to be clearer of what my intention is. Instead of "hard," I am trying now to use phrases like "applied effort" or "applied focus" and, where appropriate, the idea of being "fully engaged."

Growing up, I associated the word "work" with demanding and unpleasant effort that resulted in monetary rewards. I've been exploring alternatives since I realized the negative associations my young children were learning when I used the term (i.e., "Dad tells me he has to go to work. That takes him away from me. That makes me sad. Bad things make me sad, so work is a bad thing. I don't want to be sad when I grow up, so I won't do work like my Dad"). I prefer a definition I got from David Allen's writings. This definition of work is "something that has meaning to me that isn't done yet." That said, I realize I still find it hard to shake the belief that "work" means something necessary but not always enjoyable.

The potential demotivating nature of putting "hard" and "work" together occurred to me in a Bikram Yoga class. The instructor was trying to motivate us by reminding us that the "hard work" pays off eventually. Up until that point I had been enjoying myself and was picturing the better me that would result from the effort. I hadn't considered that I was working. While it was hot, and there was a great deal of exertion needed, there were no walls, or blocks to break. Yes, there was resistance, but not of an intolerable level.

In exploring "hard work" I came across an interesting conflict. The generations that came before me will talk about hard work being character-building and necessary for survival. I am certain that is true, at least the survival part. My generation is often seen as "always working" by those who are younger, the "hard" aspect being often debated by those who are older. The generations after me are often seen as soft and not hard workers. I have heard that young people are being taught to only choose things they enjoy when defining their career. I was asked if we run the risk of always chasing the "easy option" and never amounting to much because we've forgotten how to work hard. I don't buy into any of this. I suggest it's just diverting us away from the truth. It's like banging our heads against the wall, because that's what we were led to believe was important. Other than perspective and perhaps terminology use, basic human needs are unchanged. We all want to engage in meaningful and prosperous activity. Different times require different approaches. That's all it is.

Bringing all this together provided a huge learning opportunity. With the new clarity, I concluded that for me, "hard work" meant "intolerable resistance to what I needed to get done." That had me thinking about what was "tolerable resistance" and furthermore, how good would it be if there was no resistance. Being aware of the resistance provided a further opportunity. I could now associate resistance levels with something being not where it should be. I had the trigger to bring focus on changing my approach or direction so there was less resistance. But that wasn't where it ended. The big breakthrough came when I appreciated what resistance really is. It is a signal that I was not fully aligned with where I needed to be. If there is resistance, I am off course, even if just slightly.

As an example, I was fitting some brackets to the roof of my car so I could fit bike racks. The nut in the roof that was designed for the bracket had rusted up. I couldn't get any traction with the tool the manufacturer provided—it was too hard to turn the bolt. So, I got my own tool, a much bigger spanner. I then applied a whole lot more force. Instead of making the bolt turn in the nut. The bolt just snapped in half. There was too much force proportionate to the resistance. Not only was I using the wrong tool, but I was using the wrong approach. The thing I should have done and saved myself a huge amount of time and effort, was to replace the nut first.

Life is the same. If I find too much resistance I am doing it wrong, or that experience isn't aligned with what I stand for and where I am heading.

CIA

In the coaching world there is a model called "CIA" This model is presented by Neil Thompson and Sue Thompson in their 2008 book, *The Critically Reflective Practitioner*. The model is useful for breaking down complicated needs and wants. It has three elements, "Control," "Influence," and "Accept." The control element represents aspects of my situation that I can control (i.e., my thoughts, feelings, personal stuff, and physical actions). The influence element represents the aspects in my world that I can't control, but that I can bring some level of direction to through my influence (i.e., where I have trust or authority). The accept element is for everything else (i.e., where I have no direct control or influence). The model is useful when I need to rationalize why I have resistance to a situation or choice. However, it misses the mark. I am never really in total control of everything. Nor am I truly able to guarantee the outcome through directing the actions of others. Life is just too complex. Breaking down my choices by "Control," "Influence," or "Accept" sets me up for disappointment. This is because the "accept" is always the fall back. Unfortunately, accepting something that isn't aligned to what I feel is right eventually grinds me down and that turns to frustration and anger.

My preference is to look at things slightly differently when I am trying to rationalize why I have resistance to a situation or choice. I still use the CIA acronym and the premise, but I give the letters different meaning. "C" is for "Create my reality" and relates to actions I can take. These are the actions that will help me create the reality that I want, the person I want to be, and to create my physical, mental, and connected best self. Focus here brings direct benefit and experiences for myself and those I care about. The "I" is for "Integrate my reality" and is one step back from actions that fit directly with my path. Integrating is about combining my and others' actions into a single shared reality (i.e., where there is a shared goal or direction, in partnership, team, or group situations). The final aspect is the "A" and stands for "Aligning my reality." This is where I use the actions and experiences of others definition in bringing me closer to the reality I want and desire. It's about choosing to use the path set out by others to learn and grow. Examples would be joining a Camino walk where someone else sets the path and pace, or playing a game with enthusiasm and vigor, using the odd rules defined by my child, or embracing the potential of an arranged marriage. Actions that integrate me with someone else's path and purpose, do help me. It is a form of Otherish Giving, as explored further in chapter fifteen. This kind of giving brings benefit to others, without compromise to my own experience or wellbeing. Engagement and alignment with my journey and ultimately my purpose, can be achieved in everything that I do and experience, no matter how much, or how little control or influence I have.

Chapter 18: The art of flying

Throw yourself at the ground and miss

The art of flying comes from *The Hitchhiker's Guide to the Galaxy*, which is a comedy science-fiction series created by Douglas Adams. It was initially developed for radio in the late 1970s, and then went into other formats including theater, books, a TV series, video games, and films. The series centers around a book, The Hitchhiker's Guide to the Galaxy, which is a futuristic guidebook for intergalactic hitchhikers. The art of flying, or rather "knack," as defined in The Hitchhiker's Guide to the Galaxy, is the ability to "throw yourself at the ground and miss." It is evident to me that I mostly can't fly. The guide addresses this. The guide suggests that I can't fly because I am too deliberate in my thinking. I believe that. While plummeting through the air, I can't focus on anything else other than the fast-approaching hard ground. I can't let go of the idea of moving through the air and the potentially painful end. The trick, the guide suggests, is to be distracted at the crucial moment and then flying will just happen. The guide suggests the mind needs to feel this is all almost by accident. This is incredibly hard to do. The possibility of pain is just too great. My mind just can't let go of it. No matter how hard I try to focus elsewhere, at the back of my mind, in the dark recesses, there will be doubt linked to the fast-approaching ground. That doubtful thought might be miniscule in comparison to every other thought, but if it is there, I will hit the ground. This has very powerful ramifications. If I want to truly "fly," I need to track down the doubt and completely remove it. There is one further element to the art of flying. The guide suggests that if I find myself accidentally hovering just about the ground, I risk having my experience further hampered by self-doubt. The idea is that my self-doubt will tell me "Hey! You can't fly, you are not a bird." That message will be heard loud and clear and my amygdala will lap it up. When that happens, I will continue to fail to miss the ground. This moves into the whole realm of self-doubt and that is for later in the chapter.

Formula one racing car drivers are trained to focus away from where they are heading. Winning requires that they drive their cars fast, and at the limits.

However, coming out of the straight with the car moving at its maximum speed, the last thing they want is a brick wall impeding their progress. Instead of focusing on the wall, they are trained to focus on the corner. They literally turn their heads and look at the corner. Which, I am told, is incredibly hard to do. The wall at the end of the straight is fast approaching and it is directly in their view. The car is shaking, the noise is tremendous, and everything is a blur. Yet, they still must turn their heads and look away from the impending very hard and unforgiving wall.

Taking the best path in life, and therefore reaching my potential, isn't always about focusing on what is straight in front of me. Like the art of flying or focusing on the corners, this is hard. It's hard because I've built my reality from what I already know and what is directly in front of me.

When I focus on the ground or on the concrete wall, that is what I get. These hard places represent my fears, my concerns, and my worries. My fears would have included not having enough things, money, friends, fitness, health, meaningful work, and love. When I focus on the absence (i.e., what I don't have), that is all I end up creating more of. I end up creating more of what I don't want and less of what I do. I simply get closer and closer to the hard and unforgiving places.

My need to control things gets in the way of getting what I want. When I have invested time and effort, I need to feel that it wasn't all in vain. I need to know what I've built is sturdy and will remain in place. I trust in that level of certainty. This gives me comfort and the means to endure the crappy experiences confronting me daily. It's scary to consider that the idea that what I have built, must change before I can move forward. I cling to it and that holds me back. I can't let go of the idea of "the ground." I have too much invested in it. Ground is important: my food comes from it; my workplaces use it; my home stands on it; my loved ones walk on it; and I need it to jump and to climb. I love the feeling of being firmly planted on solid ground—it's incredibly important to me. I can't just detach myself from its existence. And I simply can't ignore it while plummeting toward it.

Focus forms the path

Our focus creates our reality. It puts us in to the experiences that form every moment of our lives. Neuroscience, the scientific study of our nervous system, tells us that our thinking is aided by a complicated set of pathways in our brain. These pathways link the sensors and the memories we have of our worlds. We use these pathways to react and behave. Some pathways are so well used that we need very little thought to engage them. They basically trigger automatically. Like driving the car home from work and getting to the driveway and being unable to remember large parts of the trip.

It is entirely possible to create new pathways in our mind so that events trigger completely different behaviours. A simple example would be changing my behavior when I find myself reaching for a salty, sugary, or fatty snack. I could retrain my default behavior to grab an apple instead. Another example would be changing the way I react to a mean comment from someone I have to interact with on a regular basis. I could retrain myself to handle the remark with ease and calm, instead of fighting back. Just like a dirt track across a field, if I don't think too hard, I'll simply follow the track, even if it takes me away from where I want to be. Unlike tracks in a field, which can be washed away over time, the tracks in my mind can never be removed. However, I can create new ones. I can put myself at the same starting place (i.e., the trigger point), and forge a new path across the field. It takes time for the new track to become my default preference. I need to make it more prominent and easier to "fall into" than the old track. Once achieved, the new track will be my normal path across the field. The old track will still be there; however, it won't be as easy to find. Retraining our brains to behave differently, operates the exact same way. When I purposefully behave differently long enough, it will become automatic. That focused effort pays dividends. It brings me closer to my true path.

Choosing to fly

The Light is everywhere. It flows around us and through us and is therefore influenced by us, by our state of mind. The state of mind either attracts experiences that bring us toward or further away from our purpose.

My experiences take me further away from my purpose when I find myself in a place of high resistance. This is a place where I feel unable to influence my choices: a place where I feel others are in my way and are to blame for something that doesn't feel right; a place where I blame others and other things for the undesired outcomes of my choices; a place where my self-talk suggests I am powerless (i.e., "I am alone," "I have no money," "my sex life is non-existent," "I have no energy," "I have a crap job," or "My children never do what I ask").

My experiences take me toward my purpose, when I believe in myself and my ability to choose. This is a place where I proactively engage in my choices: a place where I positively accept the outcomes of my choices and the learning opportunities contained within; a place where I truly believe in free will (i.e., "I am loved," "I have had some wonderful experiences," "I am playful," "I am determined," "I am a thoughtful co-worker," or "I am a caring father").

The consequences of this are significant. Existing in a place where I have high resistance brings only further experiences that create more resistance. It's a downward spiral. However, existing in a place of belief in my own choices brings more choice. It brings more opportunities to experience and learn. It brings more of everything.

Avoidance

Experiencing myself or someone else losing it is not pleasant. Acting erratically or oddly is a sign that I have lost my way, even if just temporarily. Stress and pressure often get the blame, but there is another factor. When I've been self-absorbed and doubting my own strengths, I've come unstuck. When I've believed in myself and what I can give to others, I've built momentum. In other words, when the amygdala is in control, I generally engage the freeze, flight, or fight response. And when I am in control of my thinking, I step up and do what I need to do. A simple example of this can be found in moving around other people (i.e., getting into a lift or going through doors). When I'm drifting aimlessly in self-pity, doubt, or worry, I'll hardly notice others, never mind taking their needs into consideration when we meet at the door at the same time. I wouldn't even be aware of others until we awkwardly bumped into each other as we both try to enter the space. I'm not saying that I always stand back and let others in front of me. Not at all. At times it is more appropriate for me to go first (i.e., to hold the door open or to make more space for others).

It's exhausting dwelling in a place of anger, frustration, and envy. This place is detrimental to my ability to function and be productive. And yet, it's a comforting place. It is somewhere that things in my mind make sense. Distancing myself from my challenges through blame is easy and self-fulfilling. In the times I've struggled, I've found it easy to find reasons to explain why things aren't going my way. And (I'm not being flippant here) I've had lots of experience of this pain.

For ten years or so, I struggled to get work and pay my way. While there were times when I did find myself engaged in something purposeful, worthwhile, and financially rewarding, there were far more times when I had to endure knock back after knock back. There were also times when I had to ask for handouts to meet the necessities, a process that is incredibly painful, hard to rationalize, and feels like swimming against the riptide with diving weights tied to my waist. The struggle contributed in part to the failing of my first marriage. There were times when I'd find myself totally miserable and trying to figure out what went wrong. I'd feel that I had let my kids down and not done my best for them. The impact on the state of mind is significant. It is draining and a downward spiral. Picking one's self up continually is a huge undertaking, and something that so many people fail to appreciate. I've known times when I would get caught up on a poor work situation or lack of engagement in other aspects of my life. Perhaps my colleagues, boss, or customers didn't treat me as well as I had hoped. Perhaps I found it hard to motivate myself out of bed on a Monday morning ahead of another week of grief. However it's not a real problem, in terms of life or death. It's a "first world problem" and growing, but it's still a far better place than having no reason to get up on the Monday morning, having no work to go to. It's a better place than knowing that getting up will only mean thinking about the bills that aren't going to get paid. However, it matters not if I am dealing with a toxic colleague or facing real life-threatening challenges. It only matters what I choose to focus on.

Things get harder when I am not intentional and focused on what I am doing and where I am. It's easier at times to avoid making intentions. It's easier not to focus too hard on something. I find it easy, when I am wrapped up in the fear of that thing not happening. When I have so much invested in it, I can't let go of the idea of it failing. And that, ironically, blocks me from focusing on it. When I am looking at an empty bank account, the need to secure that well-paying and meaningful job is forefront of my mind but it's scary. It's scary because it might fail and that might put me back looking at an empty bank account. When in that fearful place, I don't focus on driving actions that get me closer to landing that ideal role. Instead, I take a step back and go after something that is more available, perhaps pays less, and won't be as fulfilling, but will contribute to the bank account. However, it's likely to leave me unfulfilled and at risk of losing that job. This puts me back where I started. It is like taking the cheap seats at the theater, only to be disappointed by the experience and wishing things had gone differently.

It is said that we can have whatever we focus on. However, it's hard to buy into that because so much of what I intend doesn't materialize. The reason for this is unexpected, but obvious. The reason is that I confuse what happens with what I wanted. Everything that takes place happens because I wanted it, either intentionally, or unintentionally. That sounds like gobbledygook. So, let me elaborate. I may think that I would like to live in a huge house with loads of rooms and vast lawns and gardens. However, I don't want to spend every waking moment cleaning and gardening. Nor do I want to spend every moment working, away from loved ones, making the big bucks so I can afford to have someone else do the cleaning and gardening for me. What I actually want is something quite different than a big house with sprawling gardens. Let's explore some other examples. If I want to have a fit and adventurous partner, am I prepared to be fit and adventurous as well? Also, am I willing to manage the attention that we get from others? If I want a life full of travel and new experiences, am I willing to sacrifice the time with the friends and family I leave behind? If I want my kids raised in the idyllic countryside with lots of space and nature, and enjoy it with them, am I willing to sacrifice my income and career development opportunities? If I want to have a fit firm body capable of running marathons, am I willing to sacrifice the time with loved ones so I can go to the gym all the time and run the miles needed to get there and stay there? If I want to be engaged in all manner of community giving projects, am I willing to sacrifice the time with my partner and children?

I may think what I am doing is moving me in the direction I want. However, if my focus is on actions oriented toward avoidance, that is what I will get. I will get something that is not the life I think I want. I will get something that falls far short of it.

Giving the Attention Muscle attention

An important aspect to my ability to focus, is fitness of my attention muscle. This is the part of the brain that observes my emotions and my thoughts. It is the "inner brain" or that "inner voice" that I use to determine if I am using my thinking capacity effectively. When I stay calm and connected even within the most challenging circumstances, it is because of a strong attention muscle (i.e., I can regulate my emotions and thinking). This allows me to engage appropriately with the specifics of the complexity of the situation before me. In other words, I don't shoot off my mouth, lash out, or withdraw when something doesn't go my way, or someone has cause to undermine what I am doing.

There are two techniques I use to strengthen my attention muscle. The first technique, as mentioned in chapter fourteen, is simply the art of catching the emotion by naming it in my head, quietly to myself. Once I name the emotion, I have engaged the thinking part of my brain, and put the amygdala back to sleep. I may still choose to lash out or withdraw, but I'll do it consciously and in the right measure. The other technique I use is the idea of clearing the brain of thought. This technique is a form of mindfulness. Clearing the mind of thought is hard to achieve and requires lots of practice. The idea of clearing the mind of thought is simply the idea of thinking of nothing. This is not the "thinking of nothing" that surfaces when a significant other asks me "what are you thinking" and I reply "nothing" simply because I don't want to share it. Or the "thinking of nothing" that happens when I am letting my mind wander around the place from one thought to the next. This is the "thinking of nothing" when I consciously put the mind in a totally open space ready for the next thought or input. Typically, this isn't a place that remains open and free for very long, but it'll be just long enough for me to observe the moment of nothing. The process of observing and then clearing the thought is the activity that strengthens the attention muscle.

Like most people, I didn't come into the world with a fully developed attention muscle. In fact, if you were to look closely at my career path and relationships, it will be clear that for good spells in the past I operated with very little capabilities in the realms of emotional and thinking control. I came upon a method of building the attention muscle entirely by chance, although I now know that it was by design. The method of building the attention muscle came to me when I adopted the practice of clearing the mind on a regular basis. This is a practice that is encapsulated in David Allen's work around *Capturing What has Your Attention*. The practice of externalizing absolutely everything that has my attention strengthens my attention muscle. I had a little help, in that I was a hopeless nail biter. When I started studying David Allen's approach to achieving stress-free productivity, which is better known as "Getting Things Done" (GTD), I noticed I bit my nails when I was distracted or deep in thought. So, I used an anchoring technique to create a new habit relating to externalizing my thoughts whenever I went to bite my nails. As well as getting the nail-biting under control, the externalizing technique got me well on my way to developing a stronger attention muscle.

Training the mind to think about what it's thinking about can be done in all kinds of situations. I had some success by practicing a mind-clearing technique while I run. The technique involved focusing on my breathing and the sounds around me. I then practice removing thoughts from my mind. To do that, I'd bring my focus to the pounding of my feet or my breathing. When I found my mind wandering onto some thought, I'd give it a slight nudge to see if it would drift away. Mostly these thoughts do. When they don't dissolve, I'd use a simple test to determine what I would do next. The test involved asking myself, "have I had this thought before?" If I have had it before and I don't want to continue enjoying it, I'd externalize it. I did this by recording a message on my phone and picking the message up later. Once the idea is externalized, I could resume focusing on breathing and the sounds around me. I repeated the process each time I recognized a thought drifting into my conscious. Overtime I found I could complete a full run without being bothered by what happened before the run or what was waiting after, the added benefit being that the run left me mentally refreshed. That all helped build the attention muscle.

Meditation is also an interesting technique to explore when training the mind to pay attention to what is being thought about. The idea of meditation has lots of different associations and is often looked upon with suspicion. However, when I broke down some of the key elements of meditation, I found an emphasis on giving my attention to breathing and keeping the mind free by letting thoughts pass through. This part of meditation is training the attention muscle. To demonstrate this when I coach people, rather than mentioning meditation immediately, I suggest spending two to three minutes focusing on an object. I then suggest that while doing that, they should push out any thoughts that drift in and return to focusing on the object. This too is building the attention muscle. The emphasis is slightly different, but the outcome is the same.

Both naming emotions and thinking of nothing get easier the more they are practiced. Eventually clearing the mind or naming emotions will happen automatically. It is through practice that I've been able to manage where I focus my attention.

Intentions—"ask and listen"

Things not going the way I thought they should are often because the actions that I have taken haven't been fully aligned with what I truly want (i.e., my purpose). The Light always points toward my purpose and that guides what I want. However, at times I get pulled or pushed slightly off track. I get taken away from my purpose. The experiences and situations that result feel like they weren't what I thought I wanted. And that is because they aren't. So, the trick is to use these misaligned experiences to learn more about myself. When something doesn't quite go to plan, I stop for a moment and listen. I listen to what The Light tells me about the experience. Also, I look around me. When I am only a little misaligned the experience that I really want is near, perhaps to the left or right or behind me. What I mean here is both literally and figuratively. At times it's within my own thoughts that I must explore and look deeper. At other times, the misalignment is physical in nature, and I actually look around.

I experienced the benefits of "ask and listen" twice in one afternoon. Firstly, I was departing the airport and getting the shuttle to the long-term surface carpark. The last thing I needed was a downpour of rain as I dragged my suitcase across the carpark from the bus to my car. As I approached the shuttle bus stand, all I could see in front of me were ominous dark clouds, and they appeared to be directly over where I knew the car park was located. A feeling of dread crept into my conscious. My self-talk started with "Why me?" and "This always happens". I felt blocked and stuck—I was unable to think clearly. However, a voice interjected in the doomy and gloomy self-talk. I stopped the self-talk and I listened. I then felt the breeze at my back and turned around. Behind me were lighter clouds, some blue skies, and lovely rays of sunshine dancing toward me. I was now looking at the weather that would be in my immediate future, not what I originally saw before me. My mood lifted and I started to see beauty all around me again. The second time was weather-related also. I was now driving south on the highway, on my way home. I had caught up with the rain and it was somewhat heavy, causing my progress to be slightly less than I had hoped. The negative self-talk tried to get started again, but I blocked it, and looked around. Just off the right of my view the sun was

168

setting. And the dark clouds weren't all the way to the mountains on the horizon. The sun was dropping into the mountains projecting bright streams of light into the clouds. The colors were orange and incredibly bright. It didn't last long before the sun disappeared, but it was a truly wonderful sight. It lifted my mood and gave me the inspiration to enjoy the remainder of my journey.

Since The Light is everywhere, flowing in, and around me, it's always there. It's always with me, guiding, and listening. It's ready for me to ask for its help. However, I risk not stopping to ask. Also, to get an answer that serves me, I must be clear about what I want. Then to hear the answer I must be ready to listen. That's a challenge, as it is hard to find the space to think, ask, and listen. The risk is getting too caught up in the day-to-day stuff.

I've found amazing truth in slowing down and taking one step at a time. Small steps are the best. I've found that being my best self involves a constant conversation of specifying what I want and then listening for the answers.

With a strong attention muscle, it is easier to focus and that drives my intentions. Making meaningful intentions is far easier when I manage my thinking. It is far easier to slow down and listen, rather than think deeply about what is missing or what went wrong. Often intentions are made because of fear. I put actions and plans in place to avoid something bad happening. While taking a spear into the jungle is important, intentions made based on what is missing can keep me from my path. When I am in control of my focus, I can listen to The Light. I hear what intentions are important and aligned with my purpose, even if I don't quite know what my purpose is yet. From there, the actions I take bring me closer to my purpose, via what I want, and need. The things I do when I listen to The Light, bring better experiences of myself, of others, and the world around me.

The process I like to use is to simply ask "what intention will bring me closer to my purpose?" I use the answer to drive my actions. I also give myself some room to explore and to be wrong. I can't be expected to have all the answers and get everything right. Forgiveness is the key to learning. It's also important for improving how I use my inner voice. Besides, if I keep in control of my thinking, I'll get plenty of signposts along the way. From there I can correct my path. I may not find myself literally soaring through the air, but it will feel close to it.

Chapter 19: The riptide is both friend and foe

Surfing

Like most Australian kids growing up near the beach, I was into surfing. However, unlike most kids who spent lots of time in the waves, I wasn't very good at it. I never mastered the "drop." Instead, I spent most of my time splashing around in the foamy white water or sitting on the beach procrastinating. That didn't get in the way of my interest and passion for surfing. I might even learn properly one day. As I got older and integrated with more non-beach types, I started to hear about the dangers of riptides. Before that I was aware of the power of these fast-moving water flows, but never saw them as dangerous. Mostly I saw them as annoying.

Surfing was an activity I did as a teenager; however I had experience in the waves and riptides from a much younger age. Summer holidays generally involved a morning at the beach. We'd typically be with cousins. Our parents would bring us to the beach for three to four hours of messing and playing in the surf. We'd stay close to life savers; however, we'd be on our own playing. As a parent, I realize now that my parents would have kept an eye out for us. However, at the time I felt they did their own thing. We'd rarely interact with them, except perhaps for a drink of water, occasionally an orange or apple, and to pester them for money to buy sweets at the surf shop. I don't remember my first experience in the water—I was too young. However, I do remember plenty of times spent in waves and swimming in and out of the currents. It was mostly enjoyable, but there were moments when the sand was no longer reachable. I'd have to swim hard to get back to where I could stand again. It was scary and exhilarating at the same time.

The riptide is basically the beach's method of releasing the power of the waves. There is immense energy within waves as they reach the shallow waters of the beach. This needs to be released. The riptides are sections of water where that energy bounces back out to sea. Every surf beach has them. The nature and force of these riptides is vastly dependent on the shape of the beach, water depth, and the power of the waves. In some places that surge of water going back out to sea is gentle and of low impact. In other places, the flow of water is fast and dramatic. For the unaware swimmer, getting caught in that fast and dramatic flow can be catastrophic. In no time at all a novice swimmer can be a good distance out to sea in cold water and beyond their swimming capacity to return to shore. However, for the experienced surfer, the riptide is an essential element in performing well. Firstly, a strong riptide equates to powerful waves. Strong waves are key to an engaging experience. Secondly, paddling back into big powerful waves is exhausting and just not realistic. So, experienced surfers use the riptides to get back out to sea. They then catch waves back to shore. These surfers know how to get out of the riptides at the right time. This knowledge allows them to put themselves into the optimal place to catch the next great wave. So, for some, the powerful riptide is potentially life-threatening, and for others, the riptide is an essential ingredient in how they find meaning.

Less resistance

I love the riptide friend or foe metaphor to represent the skills and experience I utilize. When I master the riptide, or the skills I need, life becomes engaging, and has less resistance in it. When I try to do things without the needed skills, I face hardship, pain, and even death. However, I don't arrive on the planet knowing how to have exhilarating experiences in surf. I learn it.

Sink or swim is a flawed concept. It puts outcome at the center, not the learning potential. It's a selection process (i.e., it puts focus on those that can swim and turns away from those that can't). It assumes only the fittest are needed. The concept ignores those that need investment. Looking at challenges this way is an absolute. It's an optimistic verses pessimistic mindset. It leaves no room for error and learning. I prefer to approach things gradually. I prefer to test the water, learn about its characteristics, and see how I might engage, so I can build skills gradually, without drowning. I know I need to put myself in the path of resistance, but not until I am ready. I can't just jump in.

Not having all the answers is okay. It is the search that is the important part. The activity of doing, the proactive nature of looking for the answers, is the important part of finding my path to knowing my authentic self. While it helps along the way, being authentic is not about having the answers. It's the willingness to search for the answers that counts. As shared in chapter sixteen, my success with finally incorporating regular exercise into my routine was a result of the search for the answer. I had setbacks, and over time my motivation changed as I uncovered more about myself. By committing to the search, not the result, I found new ways to get around the setbacks.

In chapter eighteen we explored neuroscience and how we know we can retrain ourselves to behave differently. Setbacks make it easier for me to ignore the new path and drop back into the old. The more often I do that, the least likely I have of the new path becoming the normal and default behavior. I know my intentions influence the actions that drive me along the journey. However, I realize that my emotions corrupt my thinking, inject a little fear into the mix and that sends me slightly off track. That makes it likely that I'll drop back into my old and less ideal behaviors. The risk when this happens is that I will place higher importance on the setback than it deserves. I will feel that my whole path is wrong and not just misaligned. Here lies the opportunity. When I see setbacks as triggers instead of roadblocks, I am better able to adjust and correct. I am better able to assess the learning potential, refocus, and engage fully again.

The white water

The white water, the foaming mess after a wave breaks is really where I spent most of my time surfing. And, I had a lot of fun doing so. While catching the perfect wave is a wonderful notion, it's only part of the journey. Enjoying the white water is a wonderful way to look at engaging in my journey.

Intentions are crucial. I need to have direction. I need to have goals to strive for. However, it's not just about setting intentions. I know my intentions need to be based on my truth and my authentic self, but I get it wrong, all the time. As explored in chapter ten, I simply can't predict the future. Sticking hard and

173

fast to a plan is a mistake. While I need to be true to myself, I still need to be flexible. As explored in chapter eleven, I need to learn from my mistakes. Equally, I need to flex, and adjust when things are seemingly ok. Failing is just one indicator that I am off course. It's a mistake to assume that it's the only indicator. I also see signposts when I am having fun and engaging experiences. Those too can be taking me off course.

I experienced this when rebuilding my life after the failure of my marriage. I found myself spreading my Social Needs Relationship Matrix too thin. I put too much weight on a single individual. I've seen it in others also, were the fear of infidelity cripples any notion of friendships with others. The idea of a platonic friendship is a bridge too far. The activity of focusing all my attention in a single direction was exciting and fun. However, it was short-sighted and left me with a bigger problem down the track. The cost is the relationships with others. They get neglected. The relationships outside the single union fade away. At the time, nothing appears to be wrong. There is no "failing well." However, there are signposts, an example being the view that I can't have strong and supportive non-physical relationships with anyone else, be they the same sex or otherwise. That path left me extremely vulnerable. From that, I learned that those who demand more of me than is reasonable are better seen from my rear-view mirror as I make for the hills.

Learning is a gradual process. It requires engagement and it requires reflection. Momentum is the key. I find small steps, one after another, are best. And during the experience, be it failing, or succeeding, I look, and observe. I look for the learning opportunity. This path isn't easy. Just like trying to get a wrapper off a Chupa Chups, it never seems to get any easier, but I always get there in the end.

Getting ready—do as a rock lobster does

The process of major transformation is challenging and can expose me to distraction and dilution. Timely, appropriate and quality outcomes are more likely when I fully engage in a process that involves safeguards to protect any vulnerability.

174

The idea of re-alignment is not unlike the process a rock lobster goes through as it grows. For a rock lobster to grow it must shed its shell and grow a new one. This process is painful and risky. It is painful in that the old shell becomes increasingly uncomfortable as the lobster out grows it. To shed the old shell, the lobster first finds a rock to hide under. It then painfully breaks out of the old shell. Once the old shell is gone, the real challenge begins. This is because while growing its new shell it is very vulnerable. The rock is crucial for protection if it has any chance of getting the new shell grown before it gets discovered or it gets too weak to go back out into the world.

As with the rock lobster, the same is true of my own development. To grow I must shed and then replace the beliefs and behaviors which served me well, but which are no longer as relevant in the new context.

The process of shedding and replacing beliefs and behaviors is not straightforward. It is a challenge to face down my old beliefs and behaviors, especially the ones that protect me from harm. I also suffer from the idea that they got me thus far so they will continue to aid my progress. History has proven that this is often not the case. So, while there is a huge sense of relief and celebration when I overcome these desires to hold onto the limiting beliefs, for a period afterwards I am vulnerable. As well as a potential sense of loss or awkwardness, I also become vulnerable to distraction and dilution as I strive to adopt my new behaviors.

As with the lobster, I too need my own version of the "rock" to protect me as I breakdown and reframe the beliefs that have shaped me. I know I need that support to help me build new beliefs that are better suited to the complexity and context that I find myself in. At a more fundamental level, I also need support when I get stuck or challenged. I need the support to keep me motivated to get to a better place and build that new and stronger self. This process is achievable on my own, through reading, training, and trial and error. The process, however, is greatly aided by engaging with others to help (i.e., performance coaches, counselors, therapists, and the right type of friends).

I use the term "right type" when referring to non-professionals because there are risks there, especially, with loved ones. Unfortunately, some of those close to me might be linked to the old shell. Inviting them "under the rock" too soon can be detrimental and potentially fatal. This is typically the case if those loved ones haven't shed their old shells. I have experienced those who didn't fully appreciate the new place I was moving into. They ended up using my vulnerability to their advantage. I found real and unquestionable support in people I hardly knew, but I found something else in places you'd expect to find support. Some people aren't ready to face their own demons and will push back if we try to share ours. It was eye-opening and shocking to see who stood by me and those who didn't. With those that weren't ready, I needed to rebuild my new self before I brought them back into my circle. This was one of those times I needed to adjust how I saw my relationships. The Social Needs Relationship Matrix, as explored in chapter fifteen, can be very helpful in this process.

Riding the wave

A lot of what has come to me when I ask and then listen, as explored in chapter eighteen, has related to shifting behaviors that I previously held dear. Through this process I've seen a pattern. When I pay attention to the learning opportunity, I've found that I've moved closer to behaviors and beliefs that serve me and further away from those that don't. I've found myself gravitating toward thoughts and behaviors that bring out the best in me, when I look for what does and doesn't work.

The results have been spectacular. Searching for the learning, serves me and others much more than what I was used to. I get more done. I enjoy myself more. I do more good things for others and I meet my needs with far less stress and effort. The behaviors that appear to be serving me, feel right, and are generally much more enjoyable to honor or do. Nothing is without effort and this all doesn't mean I've stopped honoring or doing everything else. I simply don't focus all my time and energy on the stuff that doesn't feel right. Doing more of the things that feel right brings me back energy, and that allows me to do even more good things for myself and others.

To encourage and master this technique, I ask myself:

1. Does this serve me?
2. Does this serve others?
3. Does this feel right?
4. Does it feel good?
5. Does it feel enjoyable?

I ask these questions when I am unsure about a choice I'm making. I ask these questions of my routines and habits as well as the commitments I made to myself, to others, and my communities. I ask these questions while I am in the middle of an engaging experience. I then listen. I am careful to check that what comes back isn't based on high resistance, like fear, or avoidance. I do this by asking myself if what I am thinking about, involves changing someone else's behavior or projecting one of my own beliefs on them. As we will explore more in chapter twenty-one, ego is therefore the driver and I ask again. And, once more I listen. This process eventually brings me to a conclusion that feels right and good, and that is where I focus my time and energy.

I use a slight variation of this technique when I am stuck and unsure how to use my time. The question I use is, "What could I do now that would serve me and others, be fun, be good, and be enjoyable." Then I listen again and apply the same process of checking for high resistance.

A great example of using this technique from my experience is the act of writing. It has never been an easy task for me. I feel I missed some vital lessons during primary school. I have struggled with passing English classes right through university. Finding the right words and putting them onto paper in the right order doesn't come naturally to me. I spent many years procrastinating about writing a book. The upside of those years is that I had plenty of time to collect a lot of material, be it poorly written. It was using these questioning and listening techniques that helped me finally get underway and keep the momentum going to get the book finished.

I find the calm boring, and I look for distractions to keep me busy. Riding the big waves of life is far more fun, but not without risk. And, big waves are scary.

I fear I will get hurt and go under. Waves in life put me under pressure, but the engagement is electric and the potential for growth is unmatched. I know I mustn't be afraid to get into the water, take the riptide, and look for waves to ride! However, I also know I must be focused in my preparation and in the engagement during the experience. I know this happens when I pay attention, when I ask and listen. I believe the truth is within me. While I know the answers are close to me, I often find it hard to engage and look. I know the key is to stay with my own truth and not to take things at face value. I know I must engage in the waves of life because I never really know what will happen next.

Focusing on the experience, not the outcome is where the truth can be found. Riding that awesome wave is great, but the meaning is actually in the paddling out, the searching, the choice to get in the right place for the wave, the anticipation, the fear, the push to get into the wave as it forms, then the launch onto your feet and the rush that comes with it. And, it's the afters; the feelings of what was achieved and the sharing of the experience with others.

Chapter 20: Lengthening the stride

Am I doing enough?

Lengthening the stride is the idea of covering more ground with minimal additional effort. There are times when I need to run and other times when a slow walk is most appropriate. However, most of the time a steady pace is all that I require. The benefit of lengthening the stride just marginally is that with each step I get closer to where I am going, in less time. Running will get me there even sooner; however, I risk missing out on the world around me as I run. Walking slowly puts me in a great place to see the world but limits how much of it I can experience. Somewhere in the middle is ideal. Once I have the right steady pace, simply altering my stride length slightly, keeps me in touch with the now, at the same time as getting me further along the path in an efficient manner.

Thankfully, there are people who make the choice to commit to being better. These are people that strive to get the balance right between the personal and professional aspects of their lives. It is these people that seek help and for that I am eternally grateful, because in challenging themselves they also challenge those they seek help from.

The relationship between effort and outcome is never far from my thoughts. My approach has always been to continually tweak and tune things, even when it would appear to be working well enough. Some would misinterpret my approach as perfectionism. Others have suggested that I am very precise. There is definitely an element of "lean" thinking in my approach. The cynical would say I am avoiding doing the hard work, trying to find the shortcuts. Plenty would think of me as lazy. I even bought into that view for a time. Everyone was wrong, including me.

My mum loves sharing a story of when I was two or three years old. My parents had one of those traditional wind-up face clocks in their bedroom, the one with the alarm that rang the little bells on top. One day, my mum found me sitting on the bedroom floor with the clock in bits in front of me. Somehow I found a screwdriver and I had taken the thing apart. I told her I wanted to find out what made it tick. Fast forward and I am no different today, except, I have moved on from clocks. The thing that drives me now is exploring behavior. I am incredibly curious about what makes us tick. I passionately explore the effort and choices we make in order to realize outcomes. I want to know how we engage and how we could do it better. That often translates into constant tweaking and tuning. This obsession, if you want to call it that, to continuous improvement, flows through much of what I say and do.

For years the implications of how I approach my experience, eluded me. At times I fought against it and at times I let it control me. It took me another thirty-seven years before I learned how to leverage this skill, and counteract its drawbacks. Prior to this time, I would get caught up in whatever I was doing. That would cause damage to relationships and reduce my performance. I would lose touch with things and people around me as I relentlessly pursued the need to do the right things the right way, a good example being, as explored in chapter four, when I labeled others as "average."

Early in my career I was led to believe I was a high achiever. It was right in some respects, but so wrong in others. I would deliver gold. My strategic thinking mind combined with curiosity and my tolerance for detail, enabled me to produce great results. I was promoted faster than my peers and by my late twenties, I was managing professionals five to ten years older than me. By my mid-thirties I was in trouble. I simply lacked the skills to manage complexity well. I was fun to work with and I was great with challenging and single focused initiatives and projects. However, I struggled with multiple competing priorities. I also lacked the ability to say no gracefully. I would take on more than I could manage. Delays and missed targets caused problems for others and got in the way of my own success.

Those that got to know me tolerated my inadequacies because when I delivered, it was pure gold. They got accustom to limiting what they asked of me for risk of overwhelming me. They worked around the limitations I was unwilling to see. If I had any sense back then, all I would have needed to ask is, "Am I letting anyone down in anyway?" I am sure those that I worked with would have told me. I could have asked them if I have ever over-committed. I could have asked them if I promised something and didn't deliver. I could have asked them if I ever made them feel uncomfortable when they asked for help. The thing I didn't realize at the time was that there was plenty more to do that others wanted me to help them with or do for them. They held back. Eventually, those willing to tolerate my dark side found others who could deliver just as well, but with less grief. My career then stagnated, and I struggled to maintain any momentum. If I was good at selling my skills, I may have been able to talk my way back into people's good books, but that wasn't the case. I can only imagine what I would have achieved if I hadn't been too stubborn to ask and then learn some better skills in managing complexity. I couldn't see my failing and I found external things to blame. I was stuck because I needed a better reason to start looking for answers.

It took the experience with my son at the kitchen sink, as shared in chapter thirteen, before I had the reason to start looking for a better way of managing complexity. It brought me along a new path. Initially that manifested as what I like to think of as "efficiency and effectiveness in thinking and doing." Eventually, the search brought me into authentic behaviors. Core to this concept is the idea of doing the right things, the right way, and at the right time. My mistake initially had been that there was a singularity and simplicity to this approach. It's far more complicated. The idea of doing the right things the right way has to consider everything that has importance, not just the thing that is immediately in front of us or making the most noise. These ideas came to me largely thanks to the work by David Allen and his "Getting Things Done" framework. The answers weren't all there within this material. I also found relevance in what I learned from studying and practicing performance and leadership coaching. These aspects are what I largely associate with beliefs and behaviors, and the underlying values and strengths. I realized that without a solid understanding of all of that, I struggled to take the right perspective, at the right time.

The model that I share in this chapter includes techniques and practices that I subscribe to. This model helps me make sense of it all and engage fully with everything that has importance. The content here is proposed as one possible solution to freeing the psyche of our daily burdens. The aim being to get me to a place, mentally, where I can more effectively consider and manage my beliefs and be my authentic selves. From there, I have a better chance of focusing on what I feel is important, and less on what others put in front of me.

Lengthening the stride provides an answer to the question of "Am I doing enough?" without massive personal transformation. This is how I recommend we achieve the balance between experiencing the world and doing more of the right things the right way. Lengthening the stride has five aspects, "Being Mindful," "Being Meaning Aware," "Discipline", "Being Responsible" and "Being Focused."

Mastery in Being Mindful

Mastery in "Being Mindful" is essential if I am to stay on top of my emotions and keep my thinking brain in the driver's seat. Being Mindful is also an essential ingredient in realizing meaning.

Being Mindful is just, by definition, "being aware", which in the context of my mind, simply means being aware of my thoughts.

Having skills in Being Mindful serves two purposes:

- Firstly, it aids in my ability to observe my emotions and respond appropriately to them.
- Secondly, it aids in my ability to direct my limited thinking capacity.

In mastering the things that are important to me, I've found that when I'm not on top of Being Mindful, I can get drawn into the things that are in front of me (i.e., the latest or loudest things). While it might be important, it might not be the most important thing for me to be focused on at that moment. Furthermore, in my experience, the latest, and loudest things in front of me will generally have greater importance for others than myself. While this is a rewarding pursuit, focusing on what's important for others can leave me neglecting myself. This approach also has the risk of going toward the idea of "if you don't manage how you use your time and energy, someone else will".

Mastery in Being Mindful, as well as the application of the other four aspects of lengthening the stride, ensures that my time, and energy is given toward things that are important to me.

My take on Being Mindful is largely associated with the idea of being present and fully engaged in the moment. This is much like what Eckhart Tolle explores in *The Power of Now: A Guide to Spiritual Enlightenment*. I also take my views from the writings of Daniel Goleman. Goleman explores how observing our thinking is crucial to engaging purposefully.

And finally, Being Mindful for me is also about not having the same thought twice, unless it is a thought I want to continue enjoying. This concept is comprehensively presented within the works of David Allen and the Idea of Step 1, Capture. When I continually think about what I need to do or what someone said, I am burning the same fuel I use to make decisions.

Here are some examples:

- Holding in my head, the things I need to do ahead of the next monthly meeting
- Continually reminding myself of that gift that needs getting by the weekend
- Going over repeatedly the sequence of steps needed to complete a report
- Repeating again and again out loud the places the kids need to be delivered to this weekend

Continually thinking about these things (i.e., reminding myself constantly because they are too important to forget), not only uses the limited supply of thinking fuel, it also reduces my ability to keep crazy at bay. David Rock, in his book *Your Brain at Work*, as we looked at in chapter thirteen, explains this final piece well. He labels this challenge as *The Stage Needs a Lot of Lighting*. To see the actors clearly, we need strong and bright lights. That requires a lot of energy and unfortunately that energy is very limited. Sleep is the main place I get this fuel for my brain. Some research suggests I have a maximum of four hours of thinking fuel after a good night's sleep. Using this limited supply of energy on reminders and rethinking is unnecessary and wasteful. It leaves me mentally exhausted and largely numb until I sleep again and recharge.

It is important to clarify that Being Mindful, or being present, and fully engaged, is not the same as being "disconnected" or "offline". It is just not realistic to suggest I can disconnect or go-offline and still be productively engaged with my world. I need connectivity, social media, and engagement in order to get things done. I also feel it isn't realistic to suggest I can make it work by having long "connected" verses "disconnected" periods (i.e., connected on Monday through Friday, 9am to 5pm, and disconnected at all other times). The key is to manage my thinking limitations and not fight them. This is the idea of being "switched on" and by that, I mean be appropriately engaged with everything that has meaning to me at all times. This means I am present. This does require some rigor and discipline when it comes to certain technology and social media. Ultimately that means having the ability to Be Mindful.

At the heart of Being Mindful is the attention muscle, as explored in chapter eighteen. Without the ability to pay attention to my thinking I'd be lost when it comes to Being Mindful.

The benefits of Being Mindful, or mastery of building the attention muscle, go far beyond emotional intelligence and just keeping crazy at bay. Having the ability to manage my thinking is a crucial element in doing stuff. As David Rock presents in his paper on insights, my conscious capacity is miniscule in comparison to my unconscious capacity. He suggests that while it seems unlikely that I can control when I have an insight, it's now very clear that I can dramatically increase the likelihood that an insight will emerge. This is an aspect I call "Being Focused", which we'll review further in the chapter.

Mastery in Being Meaning aware

Mastery in "Being Meaning Aware" is necessary in order to prioritize where I focus my attention. It also aids me in processing my emotions and making

184

decisions about them. The latter being an essential ingredient in keeping my attention where I want it.

Being Meaning Aware is the ability to isolate the level of importance.

Having skills in Being Meaning Aware serves two purposes:

- Firstly, it aids in my ability to know how to best use my limited time and energy.
- Secondly, it aids in my ability to respond appropriately to my emotions.

I make decisions all the time. To make decisions I draw on my beliefs, I consider context, and I use my experiences. To speed things up, I often form habits around decisions I make frequently so I don't need to rethink them each time. These habits give me some space to tackle the frequently occurring new things that require me to consider and make choices about. These new things are in what I see, smell, feel, touch, and hear. Furthermore, the things I already know, bounce around my head, and create opportunities for more choices. The quality of the life I create (i.e., where I put myself and what I do when I am there), is directly related to my ability to make good choices. Being Meaning Aware is the construct or premise on which I make my choices. Mastery in Being Meaning Aware enables me to make the choices that have me doing more of the right things in the right way.

My take on the idea of Being Meaning Aware has its origins in David Allen's idea of "Step 2, Clarify." However, I quickly discovered that there is more to it than just following a workflow. I now consider "Step 2, Clarify" crosses over into the skill I refer to as being disciplined. The aspect that I found has greater impact here is the idea of knowing my values and strengths, and therefore knowing the basis on which I really make decisions. For me the breakthrough in understanding came when I considered David Allen's Step 2, Clarify, in the context of Essentialism, a concept that is wonderfully articulated by Greg McKeown . Essentialism gave me the perspective I needed to better understand how I was making decisions about where I put myself and what I did when I got there.

The Being Meaning Aware acid test, for me, is that when a request arrives or when I have a thought, I can answer it immediately with a yes or no. That is, I don't procrastinate or deliberate over the answer. This is where it is immediately clear to me if I will or won't engage with the request. The awareness may be qualified, but it will be clear. For example, I might answer with "yes" and qualify it with, "but not until next month." Equally, I might answer with a "No" and qualify it with, "I need more information about xyz before I will do this." When delivering a "no" to others requesting something of me, I might use a Graceful No as outlined by McGowen. I'll get to more of that shortly. All these are still clear and immediate decisions. The speed at which I can answer with a clear answer, is the test. This is because, if I have been diligently applying the ideas of Being Meaning Aware, I am already in touch with my priorities and goals, and also appropriately engaged with everything else that already has importance to me.

To be really meaning aware I need to have a great relationship with "Yes" and "No". This idea speaks largely to the decision and processing workflow proposed in David Allen's second step, Clarify. The workflow starts with the question of "What is it?" This question primes my mind around the level of importance. The next question is "Is it Actionable?" There are only two choices at this point, "yes" or "no." The "yes" choice implies that I will apply discipline and take responsibility for moving this forward immediately. The "no" implies that I will not apply discipline or take responsibility for moving this forward. The "no" choice suggest there is no need to spend further precious mental thinking capacity and qualify it further. I have since come to appreciate that "yes" and "no" can be looked at slightly differently.

Firstly, I appreciate perspective has an impact and that gives me room to say no, as per McGowen's Graceful No. This is where I leave a request elsewhere, with the requester, or with the community where that thing originated. An example being, where I pause for longer than I would normally in the hope the requester will take the hint and withdraw the request. Another example would be where I say "yes, if you do xyz first." Another example would be if I say, "I can't help, but so-and-so might if you ask them." And one final example being if I was to say, "I can't right now, but I might be able to when I finish xyz." The

Graceful No is a "no" from my perspective but a "yes" from the perspective of the person asking. Leaving it somewhere else or leaving it to someone else to progress, doesn't mean I can't be involved, but I am putting the ownership for applying discipline and taking responsibility somewhere else.

Secondly, I appreciate time has an impact on "yes" and "no." That is, I might decide something has importance to me, but I'm not going to move it forward until next summer. This is in a way a "Yes", but also a "No." Ultimately, this choice is down to the level of importance and the context of my current situation.

The answer to the question of "how do I get better at understanding the level of importance" is simply, "know your values and strengths." By values and strengths, I mean the core of our personality as looked at in chapter thirteen.

Mastery in Being Meaning Aware is very much like Being Mindful, in that it's not a tangible skill. Mastery at Being Meaning Aware doesn't show up like striking the ball to get that winning goal or finding the words that close the sale. Mastery is only evident over time, in that I see it by looking back on what I did, and also feeling it in the moments when I put myself in the right place. Unfortunately, and just like Being Mindful, if I didn't master Being Meaning Aware my ability to be Disciplined, Responsible, and Focused, would have been vastly compromised and in some cases completely in vain. The key is to build mastery in all five aspects. The key is to understand that it takes time. And, more so than the others, achieving Mastery in Being Meaning Aware is best achieved with assistance from someone else, like a certified coach.

Mastery in Discipline

Mastery in "Discipline" is clearly important if I want to perform at my best. I use this skill to make efficient use of my thinking capacity.

Discipline is important because if not applied, I risk underutilizing my two most precious resources—time and energy. Neglecting to use my available time and energy in the most meaningful manner makes it much harder to live up to my expectations and choose the path that I want.

David Allen describes the idea behind Discipline when he explores stage three, Organize. Allen looks at the idea that outcomes of my decisions must be externalized (i.e., recorded/written down). And that I must externalize to places that I trust so that the things that have meaning for me are available to me when I need them. This is the idea that the things that have meaning are where they need to be when they need to be there. This is the definition I often use for the idea of "being organized." Chris Bailey, in his work relating to productivity, does a great job of articulating this risk of borrowing from my future self. This is the idea that when I procrastinate or lack discipline, I am creating work for myself in the future, or worst still, someone else. For example, when I come in from an adventure and dump the equipment in a pile, I am creating work for myself when I need it next. Another example would be dropping or saving a report haphazardly somewhere and then having to spend time later trying to find it again. As Allen puts it, the idea here is to consider things "when they show up, not when they blow up." We aren't talking about doing everything as it shows up. No, the art of discipline in this context is simply that for things that have meaning, I do whatever is required now to ensure that I can do what is required later.

Some more examples of where discipline applies:

- I create the space where I can work deeply (i.e., I switch off devices, disable popup notifications, resist the temptation to check for email and social media updates).
- I create the means to save the outcomes of my thinking, both physical, and electronic.
- I organize the outcomes of my decisions (i.e., the results of Being Meaning Aware).
- I capture thoughts as they occur to me, and not let them fester in my mind.

I put things where they belong, so I can find them easily, later.

To apply the skill of Discipline I need to be doing the following:

Aspect 1: Maintaining a list of intentions, (i.e., Projects).

An intention is something I am committed to doing now. David Allen uses the term "project." Allen suggests that a project is something that has more than one step, where the steps are not self-evident from the outcome and where that outcome is expected to be realized in a year or less. By self-evident I understand that the steps needed to realize the outcome are already well understood and don't require any real thought. Some self-evident examples might be: (1) fill the stapler (assuming you have a well-stocked stationery cupboard); (2) mow the lawn (assuming you have a lawn and a mower); and (3) Collect Mum & Dad from the airport. The steps here should be self-evident, so there is no need to maintain a separate project listing. Anything longer than a year is really a Goal or a Focus.

Aspect 2: Maintaining lists of decisions, I've made about what I will do (i.e., a list of next actions).

A next action is something that I can do now, or anytime from now, and that will move a project closer to achieving the desired outcome. In the past, I would have confused "Tasks" with next actions. For example, I can't "do" a "Weekly Report", that is a task. I can, however, "Open last week's report and prepare it for making changes," as that is a specific action that I can do now.

Aspect 3: Maintaining accurate records of date and time commitments, (i.e., calendar diaries).

It sounds obvious, but it always surprises me how much people rely on their memories for date and time commitments they have made. This is not so much the case in a work context, but when it came to personal commitments, I would have tended to let myself down. As things get complex, with the significant other, and kids, it is just unrealistic that I will remember every date and time I have committed to doing something for myself or with others.

Aspect 4: Maintaining a later start list.

A later start list is a list of things that I can't start now, or it doesn't make sense to start now. For example, "renew passport" is not something that makes sense to start just after I've got a new passport. But it will be something important to do as the current passport approaches its expiry date.

Aspect 5: Maintaining a list of things, I am not going to do right now.

If I am mastering Being Meaning Aware, it will be easy to know what I will do now and what I won't. However, I will struggle to let go of it unless I am sure that I will get back to it at some point. David Allen refers to this as a "Someday Maybe List". I prefer the idea of "Deferred Decisions". Either way, this list is for those things that are important in that they have meaning for me, but not just right now given the other things I know about that need my attention.

Aspect 6: At predefined intervals, looking in all the places I have collected stuff and apply my Being Meaning Aware skills.

At regular intervals, perhaps daily, I must review things I have captured. I am constantly coming across new stuff and that stuff needs to be processed. That stuff would include physical things, emails, social media updates, news, other forms of instant messaging and of course, thoughts. Each one of these new things may be important to me. I need to apply discipline to ensure I spend time deciding what these things mean. I need to consider if I am going to do something with them. Regular and frequent attention to processing is important because if the piles get too big, I won't go near them anymore.

Unfortunately, when it comes to mastery in this aspect, the devil is in the detail. Sometimes I just have to roll up my sleeves and get it done. Achieving mastery in the skill of Discipline is largely about forming habits. I won't do it just with a desire to be more disciplined. To be more disciplined I must trick myself with reminders and external accountability to keep up the required rigor.

Mastery in Being Responsible

Mastery in "Being Responsible" ensures I am appropriately engaged with the decisions I've made about what is important. In other words, I reflect on and review the thinking I have already done so I don't forget to follow through on commitments to myself and others.

While the whole idea of lengthening the stride can't be realized without mastery of all five skills, the skill of "Being Responsible" is crucial and is the aspect that is often the hardest to apply and master.

Having a healthy mind and body and delivering meaning (i.e., being the best that I can be), takes time and effort. I need to really apply myself to make the real changes that will drive me forward and keep up the momentum. Being Responsible is about me being accountable to myself for the decisions I have already made. I run the risk of all my efforts being in vain if I don't take that responsibility seriously. I stand to waste all my effort on capturing what has my attention, making decisions about what is important and organizing those decisions. On the other hand, taking responsibility for what I decide increases my chances of my being my true self. It increases my chances of my looking after myself and putting myself where I need to be when I need to be there. Once I do that, I can deliver meaning (i.e., help myself and others have happier and more engaging lives).

David Allen describes the idea behind Being Responsible when he explores step 4, Reflect. When I first learned about GTD, this fourth step confused me until I realized that "Reflect" wasn't a passive activity as I had been conditioned to believe. It wasn't just about heading off to a quiet place to think deeply about all that is and could be. No, I came to understand that "Reflect" was a very tactical part of the system that was used constantly throughout the day. GTD brings a lot of attention to weekly activities around reviewing commitments and the progress being made. GTD also makes mention of the decision process we go through every other moment of the week when we face choices about what to do next or if to stop something. However, when I tried practicing this step, I always fell short of the behaviors that I felt were needed. Over time I realized it wasn't the system that was letting me down, it was my motivation. I didn't have the correct lever associated with this part of the system. Once I started understanding values and their relationship to motivation to make changes, I realized this step was about taking responsibility. Once that was firmly grounded into my psyche it became easier to uphold the behaviors, I knew I needed. After this insight, I found it much easier to make choices about what I would do, as well as know when it was appropriate to start or stop something. I found I was more regularly and more consistently reviewing all the decisions I had taken. These regular reviews made me feel more confident that what I chose to do at any given moment was the most important thing to be doing at that moment.

To apply the skill of Being Responsible I need to be doing the following:

Step 1: Using my lists.

It sounds kind of obvious, but often, when I find myself frustrated with lack of progress or having a feeling of under-achieving, it is because I have not used my lists of decisions. Instead, I have just gone and done what is on my mind. All the effort put into Being Mindful, Being Meaning Aware and Discipline is totally in vain if I don't use the outcomes of those activities. To use the lists, I read them at any point where my next activity isn't set by a time commitment (i.e., a calendar entry). Instead of just doing what I have in my head, which if skill one is being used, should be nothing, I read the lists. The thing that is screaming "do me now" may be the right thing to do now, but it might not be.

I now appreciate that I will never have enough time in my life, no matter where I am in the journey, to do everything I should, could, need, or want to do. The list of things to do will always be longer than the amount of time I have. The key is to have an efficient process to get to the bottom of what is the most important thing to be doing at any given moment, so that I can be certain my time is being used properly. Once I have this efficient process in use, I will reach choice without burden. This means I will be doing the most important thing to be doing at that moment and hold no guilt or regret about what I am not doing.

Using my lists ensures I am choosing the most important thing to be doing at any given moment.

Step 2: Being realistic

To achieve the benefits of choosing the right thing to be doing at any given moment: firstly, I need to finish my thinking about things I want to do (i.e., Being Meaning Aware). Then I need to organize the results of that thinking (i.e., Discipline). And finally, I need to make time to use this thinking to make decisions about what I will do at any given moment. That decision process involves three parts. Firstly, I need to consider the context I find myself (i.e., trying to do actions that require an internet connection when I am at 35,000 feet in Economy is only going to wreck my head). Secondly, I need to look at how much time I have before the next time-based commitment (i.e., there is no point starting something that takes sixty minutes if I only have thirty minutes before the next meeting). Finally, I need to consider my resources, my energy, and attention (i.e., there is no point starting something that requires good concentration when I've just come out of a mentally draining conversation).

When I consider "context", "time available" and "energy", I am better placed to know very quickly which of the things on my lists is the most important thing to be doing at that moment.

David Allen explores these ideas within stage 3, Organize.

Step 3: Cleaning as I go.

Completing actions is crucial to achieving my goals; however, losing track of where I am with respect to all associated actions will slow me down. It is important, therefore, that when I finish one action, I close the loop, and update my lists with the next action. This housekeeping activity is part of the skill of Discipline; however, it is the skill of Being Responsible that will ensure I update the lists and therefore don't forget.

Periodically, perhaps weekly, I must clean up my list of actions. When I get busy, I take short cuts. I don't always apply the discipline I need to apply. My list of things to do can become less than effective. I find there are two things that cause me to avoid using my lists of decisions. Firstly, I have written down a "task" to save time, when I should take a few moments more and qualify what is the actual next physical thing that will move this forward. These "tasks" don't get done, because my mind goes into overdrive every time, I read them. The second reason my lists need cleaning up is because the level of importance has changed (i.e., while it was important when I wrote the item on the list, it is no longer as important as other things I decided I will do).

Periodically, perhaps weekly, I must look over the list of commitments I have made to myself, to others, and those which others have made to me. These commitments should be maintained in a list of intentions, or projects, and delegated lists as outlined when I wrote about skill 3, Discipline. Reviewing these lists ensures that I have a good sense of the bigger picture. As the week progresses, I might find I have completed an action or two and forgot to add the next action onto my lists. Reviewing the list of intentions provides the opportunity to catch things that may be about to fall between the gaps or leave me missing a commitment to someone else. This regular review also provides the space to remind myself of commitments that have been made by others and gives me the opportunity to follow-up again.

I must do regular housekeeping on my filing (i.e., monthly or quarterly). In supporting the commitments that I make, I will accumulate stuff. This stuff includes physical things, emails, social media updates, news, other forms of instant messaging and, of course, thoughts. All these things are stored somewhere, even if just temporarily while I use them. If I don't regularly purge these places, they get too full and cumbersome and once that happens, I don't use them, or I will just pile more stuff on top.

Being Responsible is by far the hardest skill to master. With better motivation that comes from understanding who I am, mastery is easier but still not guaranteed. The problem relates to habits and the way the chemicals in our brains react to what we are doing. Chris Bailey, in his book *The Productivity Project: Proven Ways to Become more Awesome*, presents these challenges in an easy to grasp and entertaining way. In summary, the chemicals (i.e., "brain fuel"), that are used for thinking and organizing, are also used to do something enjoyable and have fun. This makes it hard for us to change ourselves to be doing the things we know are better for us, when there are plenty of just as enjoyable activities beckoning for our attention.

The key to mastery of Being Responsible is accepting I am human, that willpower isn't enough, and to use external triggers and accountability levers to build the habits I need. I will explore this further in chapter twenty-one.

Mastery in Being Focused

Mastery in "Being Focused" is crucial to achieving anything close to authenticity. Focus is the essential skill in seizing the moment. Focus is the thing that allows me to experience my potential. It is crucial in creating the wonderful things I am capable of sharing with the world.

Focus is about staying on task for the time it requires, be it minutes, or hours. And that takes energy. Using energy effectively requires knowledge. I needed a deep understanding of what I was good at (i.e., my stronger strengths). Things that I am good at raise my energy, while other things deplete it.

Focus is also about reducing distraction and training my mind to do that. I like the way Chris Bailey outlines the options in this respect, in his work on *The Productivity Project*. Bailey emphasizes the need to exercise the attention muscle and how it helps reduce the impact of distraction.

Focus is also about creating the conditions that enable it. Cal Newport writes extensively around this idea. In his work, *Deep Work: Rules for Focused Success in a Distracted World*, Newport includes countless examples of how we can utilize both shallow and deep focus to drive our productivity. Newport also shares the evidence about how we are allowing ourselves to build skills in shallow work, by not managing our distractions effectively and efficiently. Knowing my limitations helps me create habits and conditions that allow me to focus.

David Allen's *Mind Like Water* piece is one of my favorite analogies on Focus and I guess, everything to do with lengthening the stride. Allen talks about the idea of a stone hitting a calm pond. When the stone hits the water, the pond absorbs the stone. There might be a splash or waves, or just ripples, however eventually the water returns to calm. It is as if the stone never dropped into it. Allen suggests that in performing at our best, we must bring ourselves to have a mind like the calm pond, so that with each new input, interruption, or distraction, we are able to handle it efficiently and effectively with ease and return as soon as possible to a calm pond-like state.

Focus is crucial to having the journey of my choosing. It is through this focus that I understand the true nature of my experiences.

Lengthening the stride gives me confidence that each choice is the most appropriate decision at that moment in time given all that I am and know. The importance of this in the context of the journey is explored at the start of the next chapter.

Chapter 21: It all starts here

I have found it relatively easy to put on the "happy hat" and claim that I subscribed to the idea of living for the moment. I've often found myself saying "I have no regrets" or "that life starts now." However, for many years I didn't fully understand what any of that really meant, nor how to achieve it.

The rocking chair

Let's explore the rocking chair concept. This is when I am in my twilight years enjoying the moment sitting in my rocking chair on my veranda, looking back over my life. I would be reflecting and seeing no point where I regretted a decision or something I did. The problem for me here is that I can barely remember the details of a few months ago, never mind the whole of my life up until this point. I'm thinking that when I am in my twilight years, I'm going to really struggle remembering every moment and every decision and be certain that I didn't make a bad choice, or that I did something that I now regret. I think the best that I can hope for is to have the confidence that when I reflect, I feel that at every point I made the best decision I could, given where I was, the environment around me, and the knowledge I had at the time.

The challenge is that unless I apply myself, it's unrealistic to think that I will be making the best decision in any given moment. I had always thought I'd been doing that. I discovered I was wrong. That happened when I started to explore Lengthening the Stride, as outlined in the previous chapter. My eyes were opened to the busyness and how it blocks my ability to think clearly and truly appreciate what is before me. The busy mind struggles to see everything that I want or need. It struggles to see everything in my immediate view and the consequences of action or inaction. Without this awareness I struggle to make effective decisions. I am just guessing. It was from that point that I started making decisions confidently. I had the method and awareness to know that they were the best decisions based on where I was at, the environment around me, and the things I knew at that point in time. Prior to that I was kidding myself. I thought I was on top of everything I needed to do, wanted to do, should do, and all the commitments I had. The reality was that I was only aware of a fraction of those things. Unfortunately, that was only the starting place. It took me another ten years to really appreciate the impact of my decisions and how to make them in a way that aligned with who I was and where I was going.

It can be comforting, for a time at least, to hide in our past achievements and choices. When I succumb to the busyness or when I fail to adjust my goals based on new perspective, I risk the trap of being comfortably numb.

Leveraging the past

I am blessed in that I have a loving and caring extended family. I remember Christmas celebrations with lots of cousins, games, fun, and pure joy. As a teenager, I couldn't understand why some of my friends weren't looking forward to Christmas and the family gathering. As I experienced more of the world, it came clear to me that I was blessed. There was such comfort in reflecting on those times. However, a past like that has its risks. It could be argued that I was unprepared for the big bad world; however, the most significant impact for me was that I used it to hide from the present. When I became a husband and father, I would try to recreate those fond experiences. I would try to recreate the routines on Christmas Eve, the way I had spent Christmas morning and afternoon, and the way the Christmas dinner was prepared. I found I was too focused on routines and things that were part of my past reality. It took me away from fully experiencing the joys of my new family. I've found that reflecting or daydreaming of past joys is a wonderful way to endure the pains. However, it does take me away from the present. It takes me away from interacting and engaging with the new situation. That is where the risk lies. Too much time spent living the past joys reduces the time that can be put toward facing the realities of the present. It reduces my focus and awareness. Clearly, I need to use past joy to lift myself back up after a fall. However, dwelling there isn't going to serve me.

The risk associated with dwelling on past joys, applies also to dwelling on past pain, or the pain that resulted from my choices. It would be great to be able to sit back in my rocking chair and claim I have no regrets. It is just not realistic. I can't fully know the consequences of all my choices, ahead of making them.

Some consequences will cause pain for myself or others. Reflecting does have a significant benefit; in that it allows me to find better ways to experience the world. A big life lesson for me came after many years of failing to progress my career. At the core of this lesson was the challenge of aligning my career progression with the location choice that my first wife and I made with respect to where we wanted to raise our family. For several years, I was focused on the hundreds of unanswered job applications or handful of first round interviews that went no further. My focus wasn't on what I had or what I was good at. My focus was on what I didn't have or what this location couldn't offer me. I found my negative attitude limited my perspective. I found that I sold myself short and often went for roles that weren't really going to utilize my full potential or meet my financial commitments. And in hindsight there is little wonder why I never was successful in securing any of these roles. To move forward proactively I needed to first adjust my focus. Once I started focusing on what I had and what I had achieved, my perception of what was possible shifted dramatically. With this new perspective, the goals I aligned with and the actions that resulted moved me to a career that leveraged my potential and met my needs.

Awareness, the fall, growing, and The Light

My journey into self-awareness accelerated in the first part of 2014 as I explored and then studied personal and executive coaching. The part-time study on weekends over the course of nine months took me into places that were both truly scary and enlightening. I both learned about coaching and got coached. I uncovered some horrifying aspects of how I was living my life. I embarked on the process of being self-aware.

The challenge with learning so much about one's self in such a short period of time is that some of those around me got scared and felt threatened. Instead of embracing this "new me," I got push-back. The enlightenment I shared about how I had been behaving and approaching my life got stored away and then used against me later. The process of becoming more self-aware created a whole new set of problems for my future self. This brought me to what I call "The Fall." This was a point in my journey where the old ways, context, and environment collided. While I had built self-awareness, I hadn't built enough resilience. I didn't have what was needed to manage the fallout that was happening around me. Those close to me fought against any changes I was wanting to make. I guess it might have been a case of the devil you know. Not that my failings were in anyway dangerous. I simply got absorbed in things, was rarely present, was overly accommodating and got accustom to overlooking the learning potential. Anyway, at the end of September 2014 it all became too much and I fell. I fell hard. Thankfully, the light was still on. I had just enough awareness left such that I was able to put my hand up. I raised a flag. I shared that I felt pushed into a corner and stuck with no way out. My Family responded. They put their hand out and helped me stand back up. I got some time with a professional. It was determined that my fall was owing to a lacking in skills to cope with what turned out to be quite challenging circumstances.

I was made aware at the time that most would struggle with just one of the challenges I faced. Those challenges included no income, a failing marriage, oceans between me and my family and friends, cultural differences, parenting five children under the age of 10, periodic illness and a raft of baggage relating to what I'd been led to believe was important. As shared in the first chapter, I am not looking for sympathy or trying to impress anyone with these reflections. I am simply hoping to provide context and credibility for the learning that I am sharing.

From the Fall, I moved into what I call my Growing stage. As explored in chapter nineteen, firstly I needed to do as the rock lobster does when it sheds its old shell. I needed protection while I rebuilt my authentic self. I needed a rock to give me cover. My rock was my parents, siblings, some close friends, and professionals. With that protection in place I was able to properly grow. So much of what I learned is now within the pages of this book. I tested and explored the techniques I learned as part of coaching and counseling/psychotherapy. I made significant changes to how I behaved and experienced many aspects of my day-to-day life. I created new relationships, and I fought hard to rebuild those relationships that were broken.

The final piece in this little story is The Light. Appreciating the magic of truly believing in myself and what I could achieve opened the floodgates to opportunity. It created an unstoppable surge that resulted in my experiences and learning finally being captured within this book. Even after many experiences, I am still surprised by the wonders that result from engagement with The Light. The final part of this passage is another example.

The process I am including below came to me when I found myself confused and unsure what was troubling me. This insight came as I was using a beautiful reflective sequence outlined by William Whitecloud in his 2012 book, *The Last Shaman*. The piece Whitecloud shares is a technique for opening our mind to new opportunities. The visualization-based piece starts with imagining I am walking along a track through some woods or a forest. It concludes with an awesome mind-expanding experience that opens up all the five senses. I'm not going to share any more of that; you'll have to get his book. However, I will share the extrapolation of Whitecloud's technique that came to me on the yoga mat in the hot room. At the time I was struggling to stay in the room, both mentally, and physically. Part of Whitecloud's technique involves entering a clearing and seeing only brilliant violet flowers. It is at this point I am veering slightly away from Whitecloud's visualization. In reality, I am just inserting a sequence. So here it is:

As I enter the clearing, I see brilliant violet flowers growing in the brilliant sunshine. My focus is drawn to the center of the clearing, where the light is brightest. The brightness is familiar to me, but I can't put my finger on why that is. As I walk toward the center of the clearing, the number of violets increases. I find myself in a sea of flowers that are swaying and moving gently in the light breeze. I don't feel I need to worry about squashing the flowers, they sense me, and move to make way. I feel an immense sense of belonging. Some time passes as I walk toward the brightness before me. Soon I can't see the other side of the clearing, just violet flowers. I turn slowly and see no evidence of where I came from. The flowers extend to the horizon in every direction. I continue to turn slowly as I walk and as I do, I see each flower. I connect with each one. I sense each has meaning and purpose to me. I feel I know them as they know me. I turn a little faster, arms stretched out for balance. I am almost dancing now as my feet spin me around in the immense field of bright violet. At the completion of each turn I see the brightness again. It appears as a flicker as it passes through my vision. As I turn, I feel compelled to ask myself "why am I here?" I get an answer immediately: "because you are searching." It makes perfect sense to me. The answer feels right; however, it's not enough. My mind makes the jump to the next question of "what am I searching for?" The answer comes back as "you know the answer to that." As I turn, I now see something isn't right. I am moving, but the brightness isn't getting any closer. I realize I can't focus on the brightness. I see that my focus is off center. I see that I have been gravitating slightly off course to the left or right of the brightness. By looking harder at the gap between the brightness and my course, I get the answer. I get a flood of things I should do or stop doing to bring me back on course.

Where I've come from, what I have, and what's next?

My state of mind is crucial to how I reflect on and use my choices. It impacts the set of options I see. I've found it useful to take stock of "where I've come from" and "what I have", and fundamentally, be grateful for it all. The two-stage reflection below has been useful to me over the years, particularly when starting something new or at the start of a new planning period.

First, I look back, asking these questions and writing a list:

1. "What am I grateful for?"
2. "What do I have?"
3. "What were the high points in the past period?"

It doesn't matter so much if there is overlap across these lists, I just make sure five to ten minutes is given to each list. Once the lists are done, I reflect on the answers to these two questions:

1. "What do I want?"
2. "What action am I willing to take right now in order to move forward?"

I've found the resulting actions are constructive, aligned to what's important, and are in context of where I am.

Life is such a wonderful collection of experiences. Some experiences beckon me to engage with them. The journey to bring about my best authentic self is aided by focusing on those experiences that beckon me to engage with them. When I do engage, I must allow those experiences to change me. It is through the change that I move closer to my authentic self.

While it is helpful for me to enjoy memories or get excited about something in the future, I mustn't dwell in either place. Dwelling on what has happened or focusing on what might happen reduces my ability to see the present. I get what I focus on, so dwelling on the past holds me back. Similarly, dwelling on a specific future limits the options I see. My childhood Christmas memory is just one of many situations when I have been stuck in the past and not able to enjoy the moment. Equally, the learning relating to my career shows how if I focus hard on something in the future and a specific path to get there, I risk missing an opportunity in the present that may get me there quicker or more effectively.

I am not suggesting I just meander through each moment. I consider that to be just waiting for the end. No, I must be vigilant, and awake to the possibilities of each experience.

The growth opportunity

Perfecting the art of using experiences to forge my path eluded me for a long time. It took two major leaps. First, I had to move beyond the busyness into a place where I could think with a clear mind, ready for anything. Then I had to let go of the past, get beyond borrowed beliefs, and engage in what was immediately before me. And, I had to keep doing that, repeatedly. I had to get the tools and then attitude to believe with no doubt that I was on a journey that starts right now.

To engage fully in the moment and leverage the experience to help me change and grow, I ask myself specific questions at any given choice. Some examples of the specific questions are:

1. "What does this mean to me?"
2. "What does this feel like?"
3. "What does this tell me about me?"

It is through these focused questions that the true nature of the experience becomes evident. That allows me to engage with it fully. In this place I have less resistance to replacing the beliefs that served me up until that moment. When I engage fully with the experience I will change. With each change I get closer to the path that feels right.

As an alternative I can self-check my readiness to fully engage with the path that feels right, with what I call "the Numbness Test". This test was derived from the "I am willing" concept proposed by Marshall Goldsmith and Mark Reiter, in their 2015 book, *Triggers, Creating Behavior that Lasts, Becoming the Person You Want to Be*. The Numbness Test involves answering the following question: "Am I someone who is willing to, on an ongoing basis, proactively seek ways that can help me be the best person I can be?" This question tests my level of self-awareness and willingness. It tests the commitment to reflection. It tests my commitment to taking action on an ongoing and frequent basis.

Asking "What" questions when choices are before me or occasionally doing the Numbness Test, brings me through major turning points; however, my day-to-day activities aren't always major challenges. The day-to-day engagement doesn't typically require this level of dissection and analysis. For the day-to-day engagement, I use Goldsmith and Reiter's concept of the Active Question. These self-reflective-based questions start with "Did I do my best to" and end in something that I am working toward. Examples would include "to be a committed team member," "to be a caring friend," "to be a loving husband" and "to be an engaging father." When working with coaching clients, I strongly encourage them to establish Active Questions in their daily routine. The process I use is as follows:

1. I take a piece of paper, label it "Active questions" and I write down the behaviors I am hoping to adopt or adjust, either something I am working on or something I want to start working on (i.e., exercise regularly). I leave four blank lines between each item.

2. Now, I think of how I would measure my progress by considering what question could assess if I was doing what I committed to (i.e., go to the gym twice a week). I write that question in the first blank line after each behavior or thing. I repeat this for each of the items on my list.

3. Now, I ask myself that question in the context of yesterday, and as if I'd already started. As I ask the question, I observe what I start thinking about as I consider the question (i.e., did I go to the gym twice this week?) I write something to capture the answer or what I was thinking having consider the question (i.e., no). I write that on line 2. I repeat this for each of the items on my list.

4. Now, I take the original behavior or thing and I rewrite it with "Did I do my best to" at the start (i.e., did I do my best to exercise regularly?) I write that new question on line 3.

5. Now, I ask that new question as if I was reflecting on yesterday and notice what happens in my mind (i.e., I might come up with "I didn't go to the gym yesterday because I was traveling back from London, but I will make time this evening.") I write down what occurs to me on line 4. I repeat this for each of the items on my list.

What I found, as do my clients, is that the Active Question is firstly less critical of my performance. This is because I immediately have context of what was happening yesterday. And, more importantly, the Active Question has my mind looking for proactive ways to move forward. Often, I fall short of what I aim to achieve because I fail to use measures that drive me forward instead of holding me back. Normal measures are too focused on what I knew at the time of defining the measure and don't consider the context of where I've found myself later. By context changes, I mean things that change in my environment that are beyond my control (i.e., weather, serious illness, death as well as changes in my home life, workplace, and communities).

The best practice is to construct a set of Active Questions and then ask them of myself on a regular basis, perhaps daily. Over time the questions change, as my context, and needs shift. A further extension of this daily routine is to use a numbering scale to see trends in my progress (i.e., each day give myself a score of one to ten against each question, where one equates to a low score and ten to a high score with respect to "Did I do my best?")

My set of questions has evolved over time and I ask them daily. At the time of writing my book these were my questions:

Did I do my best to balance my intake of food with my use of energy?

Did I do my best to grow and learn?

Did I do my best to capture my intentions and statements of gratitude?

Did I do my best to maintain the mental and physical wellbeing structures?

Did I do my best to be an authentic father?

Did I do my best to experience companionship?

Did I do my best to experience intimacy?

Did I do my best to be an authentic son?

Did I do my best to be an authentic brother?

Did I do my best to be an authentic friend?

Did I do my best to maintain the personal structures for abundance?

Did I do my best to maintain the professional structures for abundance?

Did I do my best to create the conditions for Otherish Giving?

Did I do my best to write?

Ego verses The Light

In managing my path and journey, there was one final hurdle. This was the hardest to avoid and yet the most important. While I will consult externally when making decisions, ultimately it's with myself that I must agree. Without that internal agreement, I'll have no chance of being on the path of my choosing.

When I am challenged or feeling strongly about a course of action or inaction, I must listen to my self-talk. The thinking that comes from these voices in my head will have two influences. The first is aligned with ego and the other is my true purpose. The latter is where The Light flows.

Ego is steering me when I feel myself responding in an aggressive or defensive manner to a change in conditions or an unexpected event. The ego-driven self-talk will look for ways to change something about that new condition or unexpected event. If that something is good and is happening directly to others, the ego will look to take the rewards or diminish the value of that good thing. If that something is bad and happening directly to others, the ego will relish that it isn't happening to me, try to get away from it before that bad thing comes my way or act the hero and intervene before truly understanding the relevance of that something. If the something is good and is happening to me directly, the ego will either feel guilty and undeserving of such a good thing or show off, claiming it for itself, and ensuring everything was as a result of the ego's action, when that might not be the case. If the something is bad and it is happening to me directly, the ego seeks to blame someone or something else. The ego will put distance between me and any related action that might have led to that change in conditions or unexpected event. Worse still is that the ego is not aligned with my path. It's largely aligned to what I perceive others find important.

The alternative is when I am engaging The Light. Firstly, and foremost, The Light-influenced self-talk doesn't differentiate between "happening to me" or "happening to you." It understands that something is simply happening. Next, when in the flow of The Light, I feel there is opportunity and learning, no matter if the something is good or bad. Alignment with The Light ensures the something is integrated into my path. When the something is good, The Light will ensure the experience is rich and engaging, and that there is maximum opportunity for growing and maintaining momentum. When the something is bad, The Light will look for the meaning in the experience in order to learn from it, but also to find ways to minimize its impact so it is less painful or upsetting for all involved.

The trick therefore is to listen to my self-talk. I listen for the conditional statements. I listen for thoughts that involve changing someone or something. Equally, I listen for self-talk relating to blaming someone or something for things not being a certain way. And finally, I am aware when my thinking is trying to justify something based on someone else's beliefs. I look for it in others too. They may think they are helping me, but it's their ego talking to me, not The Light. Here are some examples of the self-talk I hear when the ego is influencing:

"To achieve this, she should ..."

"This would have worked if only he had ..."

"She needs to do ... before I can do ..."

"I can do that better than they can; I should intervene"

"I can't do that because of ..."

"That can't happen until ..."

"I can't be that until ... happens"

"I am so much better than this, if only I ..."

"That will never happen without first …"

"This always happens when I …"

"We must do it this way because … says so"

"I can't do it that way because it says so in …"

When I sense this type of conversation, I look for unconditional facts. I engage in those fact-based thoughts and that encourages The Light to step forward. Here are some examples:

"It's cold"

"It's hot"

"I am frustrated"

"I am fearful"

"I am tired"

"I am hungry"

"The sun is warm"

"I am excited"

"I am a good person"

"I am healthy"

"I am loved"

"She is a good person"

"He is very professional"

"They are a great team"

"She has the company's interests at heart"

"We have an excellent product"

"We have wonderful children"

"We want the best for each other"

"We want the best for our children"

I allow the thoughts like that to spread through me and replace any self-talk about changing something or someone. When that happens, my thinking will focus on the things around me and the actions available to me in the current context. I will see what can be done right now, given the resources at my disposal, my talents, and considering the constraints of my circumstances at that precise moment. The Light will drive me closer to my true intentions because the ego isn't getting in the way.

The hurdle for me striving to take a path of my own choosing, is that if I don't manage the ego, it overwhelms, and eventually takes over completely. While it's important to take this concept seriously, taking the ego seriously isn't. Eckhart Tolle suggests we should play with it. Tolle suggest we should humor the ego and make fun of the suggestions it gives us. Through that play we engage The Light.

When I entered the world, there was only Light. I saw everything as new and wonderful. I had no resistance (i.e., there was no fear, disgust, boredom, hate, envy, sorrow, anger, frustration, discontentment, alarm, or indifference). I was authentic. The ego didn't have a role yet. However, I was helpless. I didn't understand how to engage in the context I'd been flung into. For most of us, we are nurtured into the world safely. Thankfully that was true for me. I was conditioned and given notions of what's good or bad, or dangerous, or safe. I built resistance around things that would potentially harm me or cause discomfort. Ego now had a role to play. As a teenager I protected myself with largely resistance driven behaviors. The Ego drove how I engaged and moved forward. It allowed me to only exist based on other's perspective on what is good, bad, right, or wrong. If left unchecked that ego and related resistance would have completely consumed me. It is taking time and effort for me to reverse the conditioning and return to awareness of self.

As I become more aware of my values and strengths and uncover the borrowed beliefs, I break through the resistance that feeds the ego. I exist in the present. I experience my authentic self. I choose. I own my intentions. I access The Light.

Keys and doors

Choice is a journey. The choice is to engage or not to engage. That journey is not easy. I love the idea that my journey is a path through many doors. The doors represent the changes in who I am and my context. The experience of life happens between each door. The secret is to know which door is next. Much of this book is about how to answer the question of "which door." This book is also about something else. To open the door, I need the key, which I know I already have. I know that everything I ever need is already within arm's reach. It makes sense therefore, that I already have the key. So, I have the key, and I have uncovered a working process to understand which door. However, for so much of the journey I find myself dropping the key as I walk toward each door. I succumb to less than ideal behaviors and I let myself down. The added challenge then as I look for the key again, is not to lose focus of the door. I lose focus as I pick myself up and return to the behaviors that serve me. What worked was to accept that this was the journey of life. I had to accept that I will drop plenty more keys, lose focus of plenty more doors, and spend lots of time searching for both again. With acceptance came engagement with what occurred between each door. That enabled me to see the wonderful experience of who I truly am. And, that is how I found my way in the world gone mad.

Reference

- Allen, David; *Getting Things Done. The Art of Stress-free Productivity* (2015 ed)
- Bailey, Chris; *The Productivity Project: Accomplishing More by Managing Your Time, Attention, and Energy* (2016)
- Brann, Amy; *Neuroscience for Coaches* (2015)
- Chip, Heath. Heath, Dan; *Switch: How to Change Things When Change Is Hard* (2010)
- Collins, Jim; *Good to Great: Why Some Companies Make the Leap... And Others Don't* (2001)
- Downey, Myles; *Effective Coaching, Lessons from the Coach's Coach* (2003).
- Drucker, Peter; *The Effective Executive* (1967)
- Gallwey, Timothy; *The Inner Game of Tennis* (1974)
- Goldsmith, Marshall, and Reiter, Mark; *Triggers: Creating Behavior That Lasts--Becoming the Person You Want to Be* (2015)
- Goleman, Daniel; *Emotional Intelligence: Why It Can Matter More Than IQ* (1996)
- Goleman, Daniel; *The Brain and Emotional Intelligence: New Insights* (2011)
- Goulston, Mark. Ullmen, John; *Real Influence: Persuade Without Pushing and Gain Without Giving In* (2012)
- Goulston, Mark; *Just Listen: Discover the Secret to Getting Through to Absolutely Anyone.* (2009)
- Goulston, Mark; *Talking to Crazy: How to Deal with the Irrational and Impossible People in Your Life* (2015)
- Grant, Adam; *Give and Take: Why Helping Others Drives Our Success* (2014)
- McKeown, Greg; *Essentialism. The Disciplined Pursuit of Less.* (2014)
- Minchin, Tim; Commentaries, Music and Poetry https://www.timminchin.com/

- Newport, Cal; *Deep Work: Rules for Focused Success in a Distracted World* (2016)
- Peterson, Jordan B; *12 Rules for Life. An Antidote to Chaos* (2018)
- Pink, Daniel H.; *To Sell Is Human; The Surprising Truth About Moving Others* (2012)
- Rock, David; *Your Brain at Work: Strategies for Overcoming Distraction, Regaining Focus, and Working Smarter All Day Long.* (2009)
- Salovey and Mayer; *Emotional Intelligence* (1990).
- Sanders, Tim; *Love Is the Killer App: How to Win Business and Influence Friends* (2002).
- Seligman ME1, Steen TA, Park N, Peterson C; *Positive psychology progress - empirical validation of interventions* (2005)
- Sheldon & Lyubomirsky; *How to increase and sustain positive emotions - The effects of expressing gratitude and visualizing best possible selves* (2006)
- Shelley Crawford; *Resilience Building Model* - https://www.linkedin.com/in/shelley-crawford/
- Thompson, Neil, and Thompson, Sue; *The Critically Reflective Practitioner.* (2008)
- Tolle, Eckhart; *The Power of Now: A Guide to Spiritual Enlightenment* (2001)
- Walsch, Neale Donald; *Conversations with God: An Uncommon Dialogue* (1997)
- Whitecloud, William; *The Magician's Way: What It Really Takes to Find Your Treasure* (2009)
- Whitecloud, William; *The Last Shaman* (2012)

Index

www.ingramcontent.com/pod-product-compliance
Lightning Source LLC
La Vergne TN
LVHW051508080426
835509LV00017B/1971